THE OTHER SIDE OF THE COIN

ANGELA KELLY LVO

THE OTHER SIDE OF THE COIN

The Queen, the Dresser and the Wardrobe

 HarperCollins*Publishers*

Your Majesty,

With humble respect I would like to dedicate my
second book to you for allowing me to write about
our personal working relationship that has grown
over many years, and allowing me to share the
details of it and to describe how we have come
together on a trusted personal level. I will always be
truly grateful. I cherish the time you have allowed
me to have with you and the friendship you have
shown me.

With love and gratitude,
Angela x

I would also like to dedicate this book to my wonderful family: Frank and Nicola Wylie, Paul and Sarah Wylie, Michelle and Simon Anson, and to my very special grandchildren – James and Scarlett Anson, Alex and Jacob Wylie. You have shared the experiences and the journeys with me and you have inspired me all the way to write this book. I could not have done it without you. I thank you so much for all the love, support and advice you give to me and in return I give you all my love and more.

The lesson you all taught me was: never underestimate young minds.

I love you, Granny x x x x

A letter from Angela's grandson Jacob Wylie
Growing up in Windsor was an immense experience. The sheer bliss, peace and quiet and nature all around you. I am truly grateful to have been able to grow up in a place with such elegance and beauty, all thanks to my granny's amazing accomplishment. Not many people can say, 'My granny works for The Queen.' Every time the subject is brought up I can't help but brag about my tremendous gran and how proud I am of her. Her triumphs only get bigger and it renders me speechless; the stories and experiences she tells me about her working days astonish me, I could listen for hours. Words don't even come close to describing how proud I am of my granny!

As I have grown up in Windsor since I was only a couple of weeks old, Windsor is a home for me, in the cosy cottage with the fire and the enormous grounds that lie around it. Ever since me and my brother were little kids, we were both curious about where the roads and paths would lead us, and we would go wandering off for hours exploring the river, bat caves, monkey puzzle tree, farm and bamboo trees. Staying in Windsor or Buckingham Palace is always the highlight of my week, and meeting The Queen is always a dream come true that I am grateful to enjoy. I am enormously proud of my granny and can't wait to see her future endeavours.

Sincerely,
Jacob Wylie, age 15

A letter from Angela's grandson Alex P. Wylie

I would just like to say how proud I am of my granny of what she has achieved. All through the fifteen years of my life, actually since my twin, Jacob, and I were a few months old, we have stayed in Marlborough House apartment, and then, when Granny moved to Windsor, into her cottage. We still stay to this day in Windsor and sometimes in Buckingham Palace.

As you can imagine I have the fondest memories that will never leave me. Visiting my gran in the summer is great. I remember on one occasion, when my brother and I were around twelve years old, every evening we would set out walking and I smile now thinking of how many alarms we set off in the grounds of Windsor Castle while we went exploring, looking into the bat caves and many other exciting places, steeped in history.

On another occasion we were playing in The Splash, which is a shallow part of a stream close to the cottage, although The Queen often goes there when she is in Windsor. As Her Majesty got closer she recognised us both, as she knew we were staying at Granny's cottage. But so did the corgis. They came running up and started chasing us. They were very playful and they soon started playing in the water. Once again words can't describe how proud I am of my granny for giving us so many magical moments. The memories will remain with me for ever and although we have grown up now, going to Granny's is special.

Regards,
Alex P. Wylie, age 15

A letter from Angela's grandson James Anson

When I read of or see my grandmother's accomplishments, I feel both immense pride for her, and also a strong sense of inspiration in regards to my own goals. It often makes me realise how fortunate I am to be related to someone so talented in their work.

I was fortunate enough, in fact, to spend a lot of time in my childhood at places such as Marlborough House, Buckingham Palace, and Windsor Castle, and I'm thankful not only to be able to have access to such iconic institutions, but also to have made brilliant memories there. One of my favourite places to visit during my childhood was St James's Park. I still enjoy going there in winter to see the Smews.

I am personally a massive fan of history; I aim to study history at university. In truth, I do owe a vast amount of my love for history to the fact that I have had access to some amazing places of great historical value for my entire life. I've formed my own memories in these places as well; memories I will treasure for many years. I realise how unique a position I am in and I'm very grateful to my grandmother for this.

James W. Anson, age 18

A letter from Angela's granddaughter Scarlett Anson

I have always enjoyed watching Granny work and talking with her about her latest design or projects. I've been privileged to see and feel some of the fabrics that have gone on to become outfits. I also spend a lot my time drawing and painting, but I like concept art for video games. I enjoy character design and created my own characters based on myself and people I have read about in books. Granny has inspired me with her skills in colour matching and creating designs so I love to show her my art work to get her feedback.

Yours,
Scarlett Anson, age 13

Dear Reader,

It took me some time to start writing this book. When I first asked The Queen if she would mind me writing another book, after *Dressing the Queen* in 2012, but this time about our close working relationship, I never thought in my wildest dreams that Her Majesty would say yes.

Once the initial shock was over, I found myself struggling. The Queen trusts me and she knows I would not write any intimate details or anything untoward about our friendship and working relationship, but, nevertheless, I still struggled.

I wanted to do this book justice. I wanted to be worthy of writing it, and to share with you the magical and engaging moments that have happened between Her Majesty and myself while we have been working together. The Queen may not have thought them magical, but I did and I still do.

During my twenty-five years to date of working with The Queen, many events and engagements have taken place. Her Majesty travels to and from Buckingham Palace, Windsor Castle, Sandringham House, the Palace of Holyroodhouse and Balmoral Castle, and spends numerous private weekends away, too.

With this book I would like to share with you the wonderful working life and relationship between Her Majesty and me. The Queen and I have fun and laughter, but there is a serious side to my work in which challenging and difficult decisions have to be taken – split-second decisions sometimes. I have to be quick and think on my feet. But it's all in a day's work. Someone has to do it – and I'm so glad it's me.

I hope you enjoy reading this book as much as I did writing it. So, get yourself a cup of tea, sit down, put your feet up, and let me take you on a magical journey once again.

With love,

Angela Kelly x

29 October 2019

This book documents the unique working relationship between Her Majesty The Queen and the woman who has been her Personal Assistant and Senior Dresser for more than two decades: Angela Kelly.

It gives a rare glimpse into the demands of the job of supporting the Monarch, designing Her Majesty's clothes and hats, and matching them with exquisite Royal jewellery. Throughout her long reign, Her Majesty has become a fashion icon, renowned for her sense of style and understated elegance. Behind the scenes, Angela has worked quietly with her to create fashion that is unique, accessible to all, and allows The Queen to reflect the trends of the day subtly, and with grace.

The book also reveals the lengthy preparations needed before important State occasions, such as the State Opening of Parliament. Most importantly, though, we gain privileged insight into a successful working relationship, characterised by humour, creativity, hard work, and a mutual commitment to service and duty.

On the many occasions I have worked with Angela to prepare for an important overseas or regional visit with Her Majesty, I have been struck by her endless enthusiasm and original ideas. She tries to make each Royal engagement memorable for those who will be seeing The Queen for the first time.

Angela is a talented and inspiring woman, who has captured the highlights of her long career with The Queen for us all to share.

Samantha Cohen CVO
Assistant Private Secretary to The Queen (2011–2018)

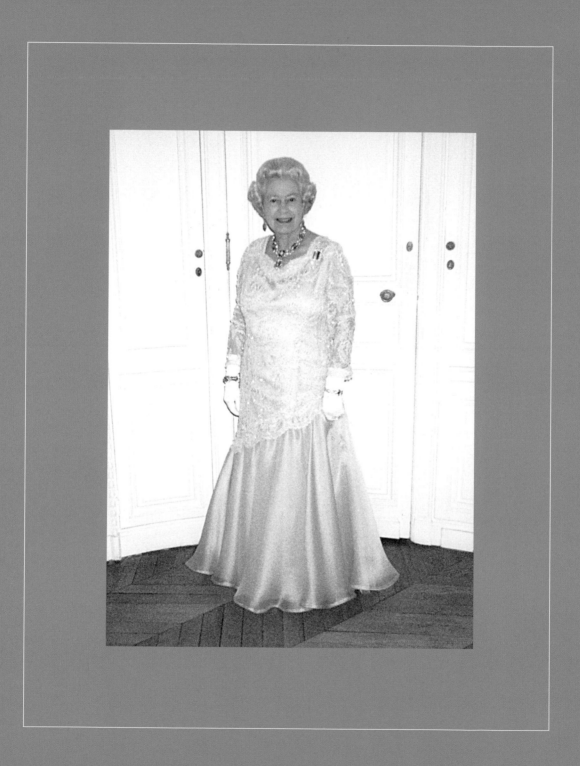

Contents

FOREWORD

by Stewart Parvin MVO

I first met Angela one morning in the summer of 2001. She had come into my shop in Motcomb Street and was chatting to our saleslady, Gill Edwards. From Angela's questions it became apparent that she needed a conversation with me. In those days our workroom was in the basement of the shop at Number 14 (previously the home of Royal couturier Ian Thomas), so I was immediately available. I ran upstairs to meet her and discuss her mystery client's needs. She wanted to look at the quality of our workmanship, and I agreed straight away.

A few days later Angela reappeared and we had a lengthy discussion about fabrics. Her client couldn't be seen wearing any of the items that we had in the main collection. The easiest way around this, I thought, was for us to pop downstairs and go through our archive: Angela could look at fabrics we had never used or had made into just one or two garments in previous seasons. I saw her delight as we pulled out tweeds, crêpes and silks – our mutual enthusiasm was infectious!

After we had taken cuttings from several rolls, I suggested that a few simple sketches to go with the swatches might help her client decide if I was the person she was looking for. Unbeknown to me, that was the start of our Royal journey.

Shortly afterwards I heard from Angela, who told me that her client liked four fabrics in particular: would it be possible for me to do sketches for each one?

I produced a pile of sketches offering three or four alternatives for each of the selected fabrics and waited for Angela to collect them. A week or so later she telephoned, delighted to tell me that her client had chosen several outfits, and she could now reveal that she herself was Senior Dresser to The Queen. She asked if I would like to make clothes for Her Majesty. After a few seconds' disbelief I replied with an enthusiastic 'Yes!'

In the early days, on occasion there might be an urgent request, and the lack of technology in our studio meant that we'd sometimes have to fax a design to Angela's office to be discussed over the phone. As our relationship developed, Angela would often come to the studio – we later moved to a larger sewing room in West London – and we'd have fun as I proposed fabric combinations, buttons and trims. I would make preliminary sketches, Angela inspiring me with ideas that Her Majesty might like.

By now Angela, who had been creating off-duty clothes for Her Majesty, had started designing more formal outfits with a team of seamstresses at the Palace. I would often pop along to the in-house workroom and offer a helping hand to ease the process along, sometimes suggesting different techniques, interlinings, and other tricks of the trade. Over coffee in her office, Angela would show me her latest finds – such as exquisite laces and embroideries that she'd sourced on her travels and at shops such as London's Joel & Son. We would drape the beautiful fabrics on stands, coming up with ideas for gowns for Her Majesty. No one knows better than Angela Kelly what is required of a Royal wardrobe, and it makes my end of the process so much easier. While sketching and choosing the ideas to put before Her Majesty, it's been fascinating to see how Angela's guiding hand often tends towards a bolder, more glamorous look.

These days we often meet at Joel's as soon as they have their latest collection in stock to select prints that we will propose to Her Majesty. Often we find we've chosen the same design. We know, though, that either of us will come up with something fabulous for Her Majesty to wear.

At Joel & Son Fabrics.

Angela not only creates many wonderful outfits, she's responsible for The Queen's complete look. It's fun to be shown into her millinery workroom, where, under Angela's watchful eye, Stella McLaren creates so many of the eye-catching hats that Her Majesty now wears.

In fact, on several occasions we've worked as a team. Between us, we created the outfit The Queen wore for Prince Harry's wedding: I designed several options for the coat and dress from the stunning silks Angela had chosen for the event, while Angela created the show-stopping hat that finished the iconic outfit.

We share so many fantastic memories of our times together from the start of our working relationship – when I had no idea who Angela was or who she worked for – to the present day.

When I look back at some of the iconic outfits we have both created, I feel such pride in what Angela and I have achieved.

Opposite: *Me and my pal at Joel & Son in 2019.*

Right: The Queen, wearing a Stewart Parvin outfit, with The Duke of Edinburgh during Trooping the Colour in 2016.

PROLOGUE

Crowning Glory

During my twenty-five years of working closely with Her Majesty The Queen, I am lucky enough to have travelled to some of the most amazing places in the world. But one moment in particular makes me emotional every time: the sight of The Queen putting on her Imperial State Crown at the annual State Opening of Parliament. It is a truly special moment for me, and I am so privileged to play a small part in it. Whenever I see Her Majesty in a Diadem or a tiara, I am composed, but when she puts on the crown, it touches my heart.

We arc alone behind the privacy screen in the Robing Room in the Houses of Parliament just before The Queen enters the Chamber to make her speech on behalf of her government. We are silent and serious, concentrating hard, and The Queen is deep in thought. When I have positioned the State Robe on her shoulders, she takes the crown off its cushion, and I watch as The Queen raises it above her head. The magnificence of that moment takes my breath away every time. I watch in awe while I wait for her to secure it. Then Her Majesty turns, gives me a smile, and lets me know that she's ready to go. And for a moment, I am speechless. Luckily I don't need to say anything and The Queen always says thank you, and I smile back.

The Queen has seen my emotions get the better of me quite a few times. This happens particularly at special events, such as when I dress Her Majesty for important events and State occasions. Once The Queen has the robe on and places the crown on her head, I feel so proud to be serving Her Majesty in such a unique position. Normally The Queen rolls her eyes and playfully tuts at me when she sees my eyes fill up! Even after all these years, I still find it overwhelming to watch her lift the crown. It is the ultimate reminder of just how lucky I am to be in the presence of The Sovereign, Her Majesty The Queen.

Opposite: The Queen at the State Opening of Parliament in 2014.

CHAPTER 1

Dressing The Queen

HOW IT
ALL BEGAN

Well, here I am at a certain age and still running around thinking that I am thirty years old – which my body is telling me I am not! So much has happened in my life – decisions made, paths taken – so let me take you back to where it all began.

It's hard for me to believe that I was first introduced to Her Majesty The Queen more than twenty-five years ago. I could never have imagined the significance of that meeting. It was my first step along the road to changing my life.

It was 1992, when I was working as Housekeeper for the British Ambassador to Germany, Sir Christopher Mallaby and his lovely wife Pascal, Lady Mallaby, in their Berlin Residence. In June of that year, the Ambassador told me we were expecting a few high-profile VIP guests who were to visit the Residence to see if the house was suitable and large enough to accommodate them all that autumn. The grounds were also to be assessed for security. This was not common practice at the time, so we suspected that someone truly special might be coming. The checks were to be carried out within the month – three months before the possible visit.

The Ambassador trusted me and soon informed me that the guests would in fact be Her Majesty The Queen and His Royal Highness The Duke of Edinburgh, with their accompanying staff. Never in my wildest dreams had I thought I would be looking after members of the Royal Household. During their stay, the guests would require bedrooms, of course, and all meals were to be served at specially agreed times. The Ambassador also explained that many private meetings would be held behind closed doors – meaning that the participants should not be disturbed, unless under extreme circumstances. My role was to ensure that Her Majesty's personal staff were comfortable, equipped, and had a good working environment. Once I had familiarised myself with their requirements, in terms of any allergies, likes and dislikes with regard to food, I felt content that I could get the job done.

October soon came around and the Royal visitors arrived at the Ambassador's Residence. I remember being introduced to each member of the

Opposite: The Ambassadorial Residence in Berlin in 1992.

Previous page: The Queen attending Derby Day in 2019.

Royal staff: The Queen's Page; The Duke's Valet; the Travelling Yeoman and Miss Peggy Hoath, Her Majesty's Senior Dresser. I was so impressed by their professionalism: everything was executed with efficiency and precision, from the delivery of the luggage to the unpacking of the cases. Over the course of the next four days, we all got to know each other well, and I spent quite a bit of time with Peggy, who was a lovely lady. She told me she had been The Queen's Dresser for the last thirty-four years and was now considering her retirement. We agreed to keep in touch.

It wasn't until the end of their visit that I finally got to meet Her Majesty and The Duke of Edinburgh. Just before our guests departed, The Queen and His Royal Highness said their farewells to the household. I now understand that this

Would I consider coming to work at Buckingham Palace?

Service with a smile – Berlin, 1992.

is common practice: they like to thank the staff for their assistance in making the visit a success. I remember what a privilege and honour it was to be presented to The Queen and The Duke. I was even given a lovely photograph of them, alongside a beautiful needle case with EIIR inscribed on it.

After I'd thanked them for their thoughtful gift, Her Majesty asked whom we expected next at the Residence. I replied that the information was confidential, and The Duke asked, slightly incredulous: 'Surely you can tell Her Majesty The Queen?' Again, I explained that I really could not disclose the information as I had signed the Official Secrets Act, now known as Confidentiality Agreements. I had taken the confidentiality surrounding their visit in a similar way – even carrying a bunch of flowers whenever I left the Residence to trick the surrounding media into thinking I was a florist and so would be unable to provide any intelligence on the high-profile guests inside. In light of this exchange, I offered the photograph and needle case back to Her Majesty and The Duke – I wasn't sure if it was appropriate to keep them since I'd refused them the information they'd asked for. The Queen simply told me to keep it. I thanked her and His Royal Highness again, and said to Her Majesty The Queen, 'I will remember this for the rest of my life.'

And the Queen replied, 'Angela, so will I.'

A few weeks after the Royal visit to the Ambassador's Residence, I was surprised to receive a phone call out of the blue from Peggy, who asked how I was. I assumed she was just being kind as I'd mentioned to her that I was hoping to come back to England later in the year to start a new chapter of my life after the recent breakdown of my marriage. It was lovely to chat to her and she said she would call me again before I left Berlin.

It was just a couple of days later when I next heard from Peggy. She said that Her Majesty had requested she get in touch to ask would I consider coming to work at Buckingham Palace? To say that I was shocked would be an understatement. I told Peggy I was still making arrangements to return to England but that I would consider the offer of a position carefully.

Several weeks later, when I was finally settled back in Sheffield with my family, Peggy rang to ask if I had an answer for her about applying for the Assistant Dresser role. I discussed the prospect at length with my family to make sure they were happy with my entering into this commitment, because it would be almost like a marriage and would therefore affect all of our lives. But there really was only one answer to give: a very enthusiastic yes from us all.

I could give one half of myself to my children, and the other half to the life I was about to enter.

MY LIFE

A couple of months after I had accepted Peggy's invitation to interview for the position of Assistant Dresser, I found myself en route to Buckingham Palace to meet with Lady Susan Hussey and the Honourable Miss Mary Morrison, two of The Queen's Ladies-in-Waiting. As with any interview, I had spent quite a lot of time thinking about what to wear. I was certain this interview was for these two ladies to look me over and check me out, and that everyone in the Palace would be an intimidating, impeccably dressed aristocrat. When I first received the letter inviting me to Buckingham Palace for the interview I went into panic mode. Those famous words of 'what on earth will I wear?' came to mind – I already had lovely clothes, but I thought that a more conservative outfit was needed. So I made the rather rash decision to sell my washing machine so that I could afford an appropriately smart outfit. I chose a crisp cream blouse with navy spots and a long skirt, and wore a string of pearls. Normally I wear dresses to my knees, but for the interview I thought a long skirt would be more appropriate. I did struggle to walk and I looked like a good take on Miss Marple, with my skirt wrapped around my legs. I arrived at the Privy Purse Door, which is the main entrance at the front of Buckingham Palace, at 11.30am and was welcomed in. Trembling with nerves, I was taken to the Ladies-in-Waiting sitting room.

As I waited, I couldn't help but reflect on how I had ended up there: a divorced single mother from humble beginnings in Liverpool was on her way to interview for a position working with Her Majesty The Queen.

When I think about my early childhood, most of my memories seem to be anchored in and around the back room of our house. I was born in a small street in Liverpool, facing Stanley Park, between two famous football grounds: Everton and Liverpool. We lived in a two-up-two-down terraced house, and it was a very happy home. My mother sewed and my father was in the Merchant Navy.

The back room of our house was a hive of activity; a place for chatting, listening to the radio, eating, and, crucially, it was also frequently transformed into a sewing room. My mother, Teresa, was a very smart, elegant, and glamorous lady, although I remember her blushing and shying away from compliments. She was not shy when it came to the sewing machine, though, and she had a raw talent and natural flair for clothes design. I'm sure her skills were

I was born in a small street in Liverpool

recognised by my maternal grandmother, who taught her the art of dressmaking when she was still very young. When she grew up, my mum joined the army's Auxiliary Territorial Service. Funnily enough, then as the Princess Elizabeth, The Queen also joined the Auxiliary Territorial Service in 1945, and was the first female member of the Royal Family to join the Armed Services as a full-time active member. My mum worked with the Service until she fell in love with my father, Thomas, and left to marry him. They had two sons, my brothers Tommy and Tony, before I came along, then another two sons, John and Terry, and a second daughter, my sister Donna Maria. With so many young children to care for, my dad left the Merchant Navy and took up a job as a crane driver on the Liverpool docks so that he could be closer to home.

My father was good-looking, quiet, and a gentleman. He was caring, loved, and respected by his family and all who knew him. When we were little, he was always tricking us. Perhaps he would shout, 'Would you like a Quality Street?'

Clockwise:
My first Holy Communion, age 7; my mum, Teresa, in the Auxillary Territorial Service; me and my dad at home in Liverpool.

And we'd all come running, yelling, 'Yes!' And he would be standing in front of the television, and a Quality Street advert would be on, and he'd say, 'Ah, you missed it.' But every Friday, when he collected his wages, he'd go to the shop to buy the *Liverpool Echo* and a Mars Bar each for everyone.

We did not have much in the way of material possessions when we were growing up, but the house was filled with love, laughter, and kindness, and my mum insisted that our family take pride in everything we did. She was excellent at teaching by example and took meticulous care of every piece of clothing she created, which included my school uniform skirt and grey bib. She was endlessly generous with her time, and whenever the back room was not being used to entertain visitors, it became a fitting room, as well as a sewing room, for all those who came to her for new outfits. From wedding and bridesmaids' dresses – beautifully crisp gowns, perfectly cut and adorned with little rosebuds – to school uniforms to help out the children in the neighbourhood, nothing was too challenging, and I vividly remember watching her work on that well-oiled Singer sewing machine. In fact, aged eight, maintaining that precious machine was my first task as an assistant dressmaker. I learned how to strip it down before cleaning it thoroughly and oiling certain components that were likely to stick. I would also check the rubber belt religiously, making sure it was not wearing out, and grease the treadle to make sure it moved up and down easily. When I had mastered all of this, I was finally shown how to load the shuttle, place it in the machine, and thread the needle.

Having perfected that important task, I was soon being shown how to cross-stitch for embroidering napkins, how to sew hems by hand and make elasticated waists – all crucial skills that still come in handy today. My mum was a thrifty woman (which I know Her Majesty would appreciate) and showed me how to make carpet rugs from old coats. We would cut the coats into strips, then double them and use an old peg to push the strips through the rug's hessian backing to form a loop. However, it was when my mum was measuring her customers that I would pay close attention. I was fascinated to see how accurately she used her tape measure, which I still have to this day, and how confidently she cut and joined her patterns.

Not only did my mum have an extraordinary talent for dressmaking, she was generous when family and neighbours were in difficulty, especially when someone had passed away. I remember her visiting other people's houses, and helping make their front room look beautiful for the family to mourn their loved one. She would take several white sheets with her and quickly get to work; I would watch her pleat the sheets and use small nails to keep them in place on the walls to make the room into a sort of chapel of rest into which the coffin would

My first paid job was in a sewing factory at the age of fifteen, working on the buttonhole machine.

be brought. I also recall watching my mother lay out the body when a family member passed away. She was so gentle and caring, and it seemed such a natural thing to do, and it helped to ease the pain of the family and other mourners.

I wanted to be just like her, so it's not surprising that my first paid job was in a sewing factory at the age of fifteen, working on the buttonhole machine. A few years later, when I got married and had children, I would make outfits for my family, but it was only when I started working with Her Majesty that I truly understood how indebted I am to the influence, knowledge, and guidance of my mum in those humble beginnings.

Nettie

I value so many people in my life, whether they be close or acquaintances. Nevertheless, they are important to me. Throughout my time of twenty-five years working for the Royal Household, Annette Wilkin, also known as Nettie, was my true friend from day one when I first started at Windsor Castle.

Nettie was The Queen's Housekeeper of Windsor Castle for over forty years. During Nettie's time as Housekeeper, The Queen gifted her with a corgi pup called Larch, who became Nettie's most loyal companion. After she retired as Housekeeper, Nettie came to work on the Dressers' Floor the very next day. For the last five years of her life, Nettie worked for The Queen archiving and photographing The Queen Mother's wardrobe.

I wish my friend was here today so that she could share with me the ending of this book. Sadly, Nettie passed away in May 2019. I was with her throughout her illness as well as being a support to her loving brother, Andre, who was always there for her.

It was an honour to care for Nettie during this difficult time, although she still had her wicked sense of humour about her. Even when she was first rushed into hospital, her humour was there. I was with Nettie when the nursing sister was asking for her name. Annette was having a hard time breathing, so I answered the question by saying, 'Annette Wilkin'. It took all that Nettie had to say, 'No! It's Gwendoline Annette Wilkin.' I almost fell out of the chair. I was shocked! For twenty-five years I had been calling her Annette or Nettie. So, Nettie had the last laugh.

When Nettie passed away I felt as though my mother was with me, keeping me calm and focused, as I helped prepare Annette's body to be laid out. I gave her a big hug and kiss. I'll never forget my best buddy. I miss you my friend.

Above: *Me and Nettie at Windsor Castle before Royal Ascot in 2000.*

Left: *Nettie and her corgi, Larch.*

Diamonds & Pearls

⑩ muddled blackberries

.5oz Coconut Syrup

1.25oz Lilet Blanc

MISS KELLY

Dedicated to Miss Peggy Hoath – who was my mentor and taught me to reach for the highest of standards.

The interview at Buckingham Palace that day went well, and I felt confident in my new outfit. Lady Susan Hussey and Miss Morrison seemed satisfied that I was the right person for the job. I would be reporting to Miss Peggy Hoath. After a lovely chat I was taken along the red-carpeted corridor to The Queen's private rooms, where I was to meet Her Majesty once again. This was where my life changed immediately. Obviously I cannot reveal the conversation, but I can say that it was lovely to see her again.

With all the arrangements made, I was soon walking through the gates of Buckingham Palace again, suitcase in hand, ready to start my new life.

My first day at the Palace was 31 March 1994, and I learned my first important lesson about life with Her Majesty: be prepared for anything. I was taken upstairs to the Dressers' Floor by the Footman who was kindly helping me with my suitcases. I was going to start unpacking, but Peggy had other plans. She was waiting for me on the corridor, took one look at the Footman and another at my suitcases and told him to put them with the rest of the luggage. Peggy said, 'Angela, don't get comfortable. We're off to Windsor for a month. There, I'll introduce you to the ironing board!' And I was! As soon as we arrived, Peggy said, 'Ironing board, meet your new owner!'

After settling into my new job as an Assistant Dresser, my first task was to acquaint myself with Her Majesty's wardrobe. Each piece was exquisitely made with such close attention to detail. I also discovered an abundance of material – beautiful silks and chiffons that had been presented to Her Majesty as gifts and stored away safely for future use.

Before long, I started to receive unwanted questions about my marital status from other members of the Royal Household. My predecessors had all been known as 'Miss' and were typically unmarried women. Although I was divorced, I was still known as Mrs Kelly. Feeling vulnerable and scrutinised, I decided to seek advice from The Queen. We had become more familiar with each other over the months and I felt comfortable in approaching her, not just because her

Opposite: The gates of Buckingham Palace.

guidance on the delicate matter would be the most authoritative but also because we had quickly established a rapport. So, I went to see The Queen and explained that I had been receiving prying comments because of my married title, which I had kept as an acknowledgement of my past relationship. Her Majesty advised that if I was known as Mrs Kelly, I should be prepared for questions about where my husband was, whether he minded me travelling and working away from home. It was time to look to the future and, on reflection, I realised that my role with Her Majesty was my new priority. From then on, I would be known as Miss Kelly.

Opposite: *Now, let me introduce you to the ironing board, dear reader! Taken in the workroom at Buckingham Palace.*

Right: *With Miss Peggy Hoath on* **Britannia** *during the VE Celebrations in 1995.*

EDUCATING ANGELA

In those early years at Buckingham Palace, I remember feeling very aware that some people might look down on me. I was, after all, from Liverpool and had a Scouse accent, not to mention that I was divorced with three children, and possibly not the ideal candidate to be working for The Queen. Even though I knew Her Majesty had particularly requested me after her visit to the British Ambassador's Residence in Berlin, I thought other people might not understand why I was chosen: they might think I did not belong, and I wanted to be able to hold my own.

I've always wanted to speak nicely. I'm not sure I can say why. It's not because I want to improve myself, just that I've always admired people who speak clearly. I don't have a strong Liverpudlian accent, but it is there. I had wanted elocution lessons since I was eight years old, and I remember asking the Ambassador in Berlin whether I could take them. He offered me a pay rise and a promotion instead, but I refused as I didn't want money all I wanted was to feel more at ease with how I presented myself to others – especially now among members of the Royal Household.

Needless to say, when I first started working with The Queen, I became even more aware of how I sounded. Listening to and speaking with Her Majesty, I would think, how wonderful to be able to speak so nicely, and after a few months of working with her, I plucked up the courage to ask if she knew anyone who might give me the elocution lessons I'd wanted for so long. The look on The Queen's face was a picture. She simply asked, 'Why?' After I had explained, she said that it was not necessary and that she'd heard about my plan – the Ambassador had told her. I asked again and again, but she still refused. After much back and forth, Her Majesty eventually told me to go upstairs and talk to the Duchess of Grafton about it.

I ran up straight away, and found the Duchess waiting for me in the corridor. 'Your Grace, I was wondering if you could put me in contact with anyone you know who could give me elocution lessons,' I said.

'You can give me elocution lessons!'

The Duchess started laughing and I realised The Queen had called her in the time it had taken me to run up the stairs. 'Look, Angela,' she said, 'if you speak slowly, it means you speak clearly. Just keep The Queen laughing – that's all I ask of you.' But that still wasn't enough for me.

Later that day, I went back to see The Queen and mentioned that I'd spoken to the Duchess. 'Oh, and what did she say?' she asked. I repeated the advice I'd been given and Her Majesty seemed content. 'Well, there you go,' she said.

'But that's not an elocution lesson,' I responded, then told Her Majesty my new idea: 'You can give me elocution lessons! You can tell me what I say that's correct and what I say that isn't.'

The Queen could probably sense that I wasn't going to give up, so she instructed me to say one word: 'furious'. 'Fyer-ri-ous,' I responded.

'No, fee-or-ree-ous,' said Her Majesty, in perfect received pronunciation. After several more attempts, I finally cracked it and Her Majesty exclaimed, 'Yes!' and her finger went up in the air, followed shortly by, 'Not sick as a parrot'. And that was it – my one and only elocution lesson, and from The Queen herself. From then on, I listened and tried my best to speak properly – even adding an aitch to words where it didn't exist – but in the end I gave up: it was just too much effort. Ever since I've stuck to being myself, a girl from Liverpool and a proud Liverpudlian, too.

In The Splash with the dogs in Windsor Home Park in 1998.

LET ME TAKE YOU AMONG THE NIGHT STARS

In August 1994, four months after I had started working for The Queen, it was time for my first trip to Balmoral. Needless to say, I was very excited whenever one of these 'firsts' came around: my first visit to Windsor, my first trip on the Royal Train, my first Trooping the Colour. But I was particularly looking forward to seeing Balmoral Castle, where the Royal Family take their holiday each year. I was intrigued to see whether Her Majesty would have time to relax – to me, it seemed that she never stopped working.

On our first night, I remember gazing up at the night sky and noticing how brightly the stars shone out from the darkness. I'd always loved star-gazing and I find it a very calming experience. I vividly recall thinking how lucky I was to be standing in the majestic grounds of that historic building. A few days later, I relayed this to Her Majesty, with whom I now felt quite comfortable to enjoy some casual chat, and told her how much I loved gazing at the stars. It turned out that The Queen shared this passion and we looked out of the window into the darkness together. She pointed out the various constellations – the Plough, Ursa Major and Cassiopeia – and I mentioned that I had brought a telescope with me, a present from my family for my fortieth birthday. Her Majesty suggested that as it was a very clear, cold night, I should wrap up, go outside, and stand in front of the Castle shortly before midnight for the best view. I pointed out that the police probably wouldn't appreciate me setting off all the alarms in the middle of the night, so instead, I asked if I could take a car to drive up to the Glenshee – one of the Highlands' highest peaks. The Queen thought I was crazy and was reluctant to let me drive there alone, so she asked one of her duty protection officers to escort me.

Equipped with my telescope, its stand, binoculars, and a flask of coffee, my slightly begrudging escort and I made our way into the night. On top of Glenshee, the view was breathtaking. With the headlights turned off and the protection officer freezing in the car, I started scanning the sky and admiring the

The Queen thought I was crazy

stars and constellations. It was the very first time I ever saw the Milky Way and I remember feeling quite emotional. Eventually I was persuaded by the officer to return to the Castle, but I had my head through the sun roof throughout the journey back, wielding my binoculars, reluctant to say goodbye to the stars. The next morning, I was full of excitement. I rushed up to Her Majesty and could not stop talking about how wonderful the experience had been. She must have thought, thank goodness it will be a while before she does that again. But every time I return to Balmoral, before I go to sleep, I open my bedroom window and gaze at the sky for several minutes. It always reminds me of that conversation with Her Majesty when I discovered a shared passion and the fact that, because of her thoughtful gesture, I saw the Milky Way for the first time.

Right: *Taking a walk in Balmoral grounds in 1998 – note the high heels!*

Opposite: *Beauty within the castle grounds.*

LEADING LADIES

As I began to settle into life in the Palace, I knew it was important to start standing my ground and fighting my corner. When I was asked to do something, I did it efficiently and thoroughly, but I soon became aware that I was also ruffling feathers.

Back then, the Royal Household was very male dominated. It had long been a place where traditions were upheld and routines were followed. On one occasion, I remember being told that only after twelve years as a staff member would I be allowed to have an opinion. Needless to say, I was not happy with this – I would only ever act in Her Majesty's best interests and yet I often felt patronised and belittled.

As I began to get to know Her Majesty, I could not help but reflect on her role as a female monarch. I thought too of Queen Victoria, who ascended the throne at the very young age of eighteen, and the responsibility she bore. Victoria ruled alongside governments where all their members were men, and although Her Majesty's reign has seen a greater female presence politically, she must also have felt the same pressure to prove herself as a young, recently married female monarch. In the face of condescension and old-fashioned attitudes, I found inspiration in The Queen and the women who ruled before her and was determined to defend my right to be heard as a member of the Royal Household.

I now know that my tendency to be forthright was a breath of fresh air for many of my colleagues, but it took me quite some time to learn the right approach when it came to expressing myself. In fact, I even became known as AK47 and The Queen's Gatekeeper, which I take as a compliment as it demonstrates my determination to be taken seriously.

Even now, after twenty-five years, I still admire The Queen as a strong, powerful woman and I find great inspiration not only in her courage, but also in her humility and gentle humour. She has taught me so much over the years and has always encouraged me to stay true to myself while being open to the opinions of others, even if I don't share them. I know that her guidance has made me a better person, and for that I am eternally grateful.

I even became known as The Queen's Gatekeeper

Opposite: The Queen at a State Banquet in 2011.

BACK TO FRONT OR FRONT TO BACK?

I've learned countless new skills and techniques during my years working for The Queen. Even now I face new challenges when it comes to creating Her Majesty's outfits, but I always keep one thing in mind on a day-to-day basis: to trust my instincts. I learned this valuable lesson soon after I joined the Royal Household, and one memorable occasion will stay with me as a reminder of how important it is to speak up.

A year after Peggy Hoath retired, in the autumn of 1995, I was promoted to Senior Dresser. Peggy had worked for The Queen for over thirty-five years, and knew all the tricks of the trade. Her standards were so high that I thought I would never be able to reach them. But I listened and learned, and everything she taught me is still carried out to this day.

Then, in 1998, although I wasn't yet in charge of designing The Queen's wardrobe, I did assist in choosing appropriate outfits for each occasion. We were planning for Her Majesty's upcoming tour of Malaysia, where she would be closing the Commonwealth Games in Kuala Lumpur. As the weather is so warm over there, it was decided that Her Majesty would wear a dress but no jacket or coat, and she chose a vibrant deep coral for the outfit and matching hat. Designs were drawn up and a brief was sent to the milliner. Sketches were done for the hat and, due to Her Majesty's busy schedule, the hat was delivered at the last minute. Her Majesty didn't have a chance to try it on and I didn't have a chance to look it over before it was packed up.

On the day of the ceremony, I was helping Her Majesty get ready and went to take the hat out of the box in which it had been carefully packed. As soon as I had it in my hands, I knew, deep down, that it was not going to suit The Queen. With a commanding shell-like brim and a very large flower on the reverse, it was certainly an interesting and beautifully made piece, but I had a gut feeling that it would not complement the outfit or enhance Her Majesty's features. I was also very aware that The Queen was going to give a speech that would be broadcast

I knew that it was not going to suit The Queen.

Opposite: The Queen and King Yang Dipertuan Agong of Malaysia during the Commonwealth Games in Kuala Lumpur in 1998.

live on television and that the world's media would be paying close attention, as always, to what she was wearing.

As the morning went on, I became increasingly worried, so I decided I had to raise my concern and face the consequences later. So, I waited for The Queen to come into the dressing room, took a deep breath, and said, 'Your Majesty, I don't think you should wear this hat. It is not the right design for you and it won't suit you.' A long silence followed before she eventually looked up and said, 'Well, it's a bit late now. What else can I wear? I must wear it.'

Although I admired her pragmatic approach, I was insistent. I told her I had been examining the hat from all angles and that it would be better worn back to front. The Queen couldn't believe that this would work. I told her that, if she did not believe me, she should consult The Duke of Edinburgh, as he always tells her the truth. At this point, I left the room feeling somewhat terrified, as you can imagine.

Before long, Her Majesty called me back. She had consulted His Royal Highness and, after an amusing conversation, in which I imagine The Duke didn't hold back, The Queen had decided to wear the hat the wrong way around, as I had suggested. She was, however, very concerned that the milliner might be upset. I told her not to worry and that I would think of an explanation for when we returned to London.

I remember feeling so relieved and proud when Her Majesty stepped out onto the stage to deliver her speech that day. The press admired her outfit: the hat had a wonderful 1940s feel to it, with the large flower sitting high at the top. During The Queen's speech, I was holding my breath – not because I was concerned for her but because I was eager to hear whether she was happy with her last-minute decision to turn the hat. Sure enough, when she came to see me after the event, she greeted me with a lovely smile. No words were needed. It was in moments like these that I knew Her Majesty and I would make a great team. I was so proud that I'd voiced my concern, and I think The Queen appreciated it, too.

So, dear reader, what do you think? Was it back to front, or front to back? Or, in fact exactly the right way around?

Top: *The 'front'.*
Bottom: *The 'back', but
so much more stylish.*

MEETING HIS HOLINESS THE POPE

After the incident with the back-to-front hat at the Commonwealth Games closing ceremony, I became more determined to speak up when it came to matters of Her Majesty's wardrobe. I had worked so hard to familiarise myself with what Her Majesty liked to wear and, crucially, what was appropriate for The Queen to wear to any given engagement. However, speaking up and being heard wasn't always easy, as one particular incident taught me.

It was the year 2000 and Her Majesty was due to travel to Rome on a four-day State Visit. I wasn't yet responsible for attending recces ahead of such trips, so it was the Private Secretaries who on their return outlined the provisional engagements that The Queen would be attending. On one day Her Majesty would be meeting with His Holiness the Pope, after which there would be a private engagement, and so they suggested The Queen would be fine to wear a normal day dress for both events. Straight away, I knew this would be a mistake. Whenever Her Majesty had visited the Pope previously she had always, without fail, worn a long black dress, a beautiful diamond tiara and a long mantilla lace veil. Having been brought up Catholic, I knew instinctively that a day dress simply would not be appropriate and so I expressed this to the Secretaries, who made it clear that my advice wasn't welcome.

Feeling ignored and patronised, I decided to discuss the matter with Her Majesty directly. I told her that the Private Secretaries had advised that she should wear a colourful day dress to meet with the Pope as it could then also be worn to her next engagement. I insisted that this would not be appropriate for meeting with His Holiness. As always, The Queen listened, however, once she had discussed the matter again with her Private Secretaries, they still insisted that a colourful day dress should be worn. In response, I asked her to go back to the Secretaries and ask them to do their homework. I considered it to be bad advice. I sensed that Her Majesty was starting to feel torn as to whose advice to take.

Her Majesty was starting to feel torn as to whose advice to take.

Opposite: The Queen and Pope John Paul II during a State Visit to the Vatican in 2000.

Confident in the knowledge that I would be standing my ground, regardless of what the Secretaries said, I came up with a secret plan. While preparing for the upcoming tour, I selected one of Her Majesty's favourite outfits – something I knew she would feel comfortable in – and requested that one of the dressmakers, Maureen Rose, create something in exactly the same style but in navy blue, and to send the invoice only to me. There would be no fittings on this occasion as I did not want to alert anyone to my plan. In addition, I approached Freddie Fox, the milliner at the time, and asked him to design a pillbox-style hat with a detachable veil and that the invoice must also be sent directly to me.

I spoke with Her Majesty one final time before the tour. Once again, I told her that I was certain the Vatican would not have suggested that a day dress would be appropriate. I remember The Queen asking if I had ever been to the Vatican before and how I could be so sure of my advice. I hadn't, but said the reason I knew was because I was brought up a strong Catholic and that if The Queen turned up for such an important meeting in a day dress, where would it all end? I felt that standards would start slipping. Would guests just turn up to the Investitures in a cotton dress and pumps because they felt more comfortable? I insisted once more that the Pope would not expect guests to arrive in such informal dress. I simply would not dress The Queen this way and at this point, Her Majesty just wanted the matter to be sorted. I had to carry off my plan perfectly.

Three months later, we were in Rome and I went about unpacking Her Majesty's clothes and arranging her outfits for the upcoming engagements. Soon

The two versions of the dress that I had secretly had made.

enough, the day of her visit to the Pope arrived and I heard my name being called loudly down the corridor: I will never forget the sight of the Private Secretary frantically running down one of the longest corridors in the Quirinale Palace, bellowing my name, 'Angela, Angela, quick!', and wearing his brown jumper, brown corduroy trousers, brown socks but no shoes! He demanded to know what The Queen would be wearing that day. I calmly informed him that Her Majesty would be wearing a shocking pink outfit, as advised by him and the Assistant Private Secretaries, which did little to calm his panicked state. 'Don't you always travel with a black outfit?' he asked, and I replied that I had not on this occasion. In fact, we do always travel with a black outfit in case of an unexpected sad occasion, but I wasn't going to let him know that after what he had put me through. I told him not to worry and that Her Majesty would still look beautiful.

He then sent a message to The Queen asking what should be done, as the Vatican had said that the outfit must be dark. Shortly afterwards, The Queen sent for me and asked if we had any dark outfits that she could wear instead. 'Okay, Your Majesty,' I said, 'I'll show you something.' And with that, I produced the navy-blue dress and pillbox hat that I had had secretly made before casually commenting that, ideally, the outfit would be black for a meeting with the Pope. Her Majesty agreed and without a moment of hesitation, I produced the exact same dress and veiled hat in black. 'Luckily enough,' I said, 'I also had this made. So you're absolutely fine.' I vividly remember the brief look of relief on The Queen's face.

Watching Her Majesty walk out in her stylish, modern and appropriate black outfit to meet His Holiness the Pope, I felt so proud of myself for having faith in my convictions. The Queen walked out dressed appropriately in her new black outfit as Head of the Church of England meeting another head of the church, His Holiness the Pope. I had known all along that my instincts about The Queen's outfit that day were right, even though I wasn't being listened to. From then on, I felt confident that my opinion would be heard.

Eventually I found out that the private engagement was a photograph of The Queen with members of the Royal Household outside the Sistine Chapel, and the Private Secretaries wanted Her Majesty to wear a normal day dress so that it looked like a fun day out, as the Royal Household wouldn't be dressed in black. This photograph moment had been prioritised above that important private meeting with His Holiness.

In 2014, The Queen met privately with the Pope during a visit to Rome. I had the honour and privilege to be presented to His Holiness. This was extremely special for me. I was holding my rosary beads when the Pope touched my hands to bless them, and I knew my mother would have been so proud of me.

FINDING MY FEET

As my role progressed, I spent more and more time working on Her Majesty's wardrobe and I started to notice that many of her outfits were made in similar colours. The Queen was wearing a lot of dark green, navy, and red, and I had also noticed that some of the older pieces – the stunning Hardy Amies evening gowns, for example – which had been the height of fashion a few years before, had begun to look a little tired. Spending time with The Queen had allowed me to understand better her likes and dislikes, and I sensed that she would enjoy more vibrant colours and some fresher designs. At this point Her Majesty's outfits were still only made by designers and dressmakers outside the Palace.

On one occasion I mentioned to The Queen that the designers should be looking at brighter colours and new designs, but who was I to tell them? I had been Senior Dresser for a couple of years and in that time had become more confident, talking to The Queen more about her outfits. I think The Queen knew that I was loyal and would only ever be honest with her. I could not help thinking that The Queen's style needed to change quickly, before she was made to look older than she was – which was what some of the old designs did. Some of the coats and dresses also had to be made shorter, as The Queen still had, and still does have, a good figure and excellent legs.

One day, The Queen invited me to join her the next time a designer, his team and the milliner came in for a fitting. I was slightly taken aback as I wouldn't usually be present for fittings; usually I just saw the dressmakers into the room and would leave them to it, but this time I was asked to stay. I was also quite anxious as I knew I couldn't hide my feelings very well: if an outfit did not suit Her Majesty, the expression on my face would make it clear to everyone what I thought. Even worse, if The Queen asked my advice, I would be forced to dismiss an outfit in front of its designer, or the hat in front of its milliner. Her Majesty would never want to hurt anyone's feelings, even if I didn't mind, and I would have to be honest about my opinion for her sake. Little did I know that this moment was yet another stepping stone for me, another door opening.

Opposite: A little colour makes all the difference. At Joel & Son Fabrics in 2019.

With the fitting under way, as I'd anticipated, the expression on my face started to give everything away and Her Majesty asked my opinion. This question didn't go down well with everyone in the room. With bated breath they all turned to me for my answer and waited, and I could see the shock across their faces as I told them my thoughts: the hats were too masculine and their patterns too large. In terms of the outfits, The Queen needed something more chic, fitted and elegant. There was a shocked silence in the room after I spoke. I suspected that I would never be invited back, and I imagine the designer and milliner hoped as much, but Her Majesty continued to request my presence at fittings, to the dread of those designers. I became their worst nightmare.

I vividly remember one fitting where The Queen was draped in a very large piece of bold, jacquard material in a large print. Even a six-foot-tall model would have struggled to pull off something like that, and it absolutely drowned Her Majesty. Once again, I could not hide my disapproval when Her Majesty asked my thoughts. Without hesitation, I said, 'No way! It doesn't suit you at all and it is totally the wrong pattern.' An awkward silence and an icy atmosphere descended on the room. Everyone in sequence turned their heads towards me with what felt like daggers in their eyes, except for The Queen who stared straight ahead and goodness knows what she was thinking. The atmosphere was ice cold. Just at that moment, The Duke of Edinburgh happened to walk past and Her Majesty asked what he thought of the material, knowing that, like mine, his feedback is always honest. 'Is that the new material for the sofa?' he joked, before continuing on his way. I excused myself, left the room, and privately punched the air with delight. I composed myself, then walked back into the dressing room where I noticed the material was being folded and put away unused. The Queen was thanking the designers and the milliner for their time and they left the room.

Shortly after that fitting, and experiencing my honesty, Her Majesty asked me to draw some of my own designs for what I thought she should wear. I told

Her Majesty wore this for her 90th birthday in Windsor in 2016.

her I couldn't – it had been a long time since I had sketched any outfits. 'If I wanted an artist, I would hire one,' The Queen said jokingly. And with that, I began rummaging through the parcels of gift materials, taking samples to show Her Majesty the wealth of beautiful silks and glorious patterns that she already had in her stockroom. Then I showed her some quickly drawn sketches of more fitted, stylish pieces. Thanks to my mum, I'd already had extensive training on the necessary skills but I was a little out of practice. I needed to refresh my memory quickly, considering that it was Her Majesty's outfits I would be working on. Each was inspired by my own love of fashion and my mother's elegant wardrobe – her perfectly tailored skirts and jackets. Sometimes I channelled the sensibility of my aunt Edwina – a designer, tailor, and dressmaker, who liked to dress more daringly. She was the first woman I saw in a transparent black chiffon blouse. The Queen saw my drawings of the designs, along with samples of the beautiful materials already being stored upstairs, and accepted them. The Queen liked the designs and suggested that we employ a machinist to help me. Before long, Her Majesty's wardrobe was being revitalised as, piece by piece, vibrant colours and stylish cuts made their way onto the rails. More to the point, The Queen was happy. It is an honour to be the first ever in-house Designer to Her Majesty The Queen.

I could not hide my disapproval when her Majesty asked my thoughts.

THE QUEEN'S JEWELLERY

Before long, my role as Senior Dresser and Designer for Her Majesty evolved. Owing to the strength of my relationship with The Queen and the mutual respect we shared, in 1998 I was given the additional titles of Personal Advisor and Curator to Her Majesty The Queen. I still continued to design outfits for Her Majesty, and did this mainly in the evenings and at weekends. As Personal Advisor, I am in the privileged position of not only advising The Queen on her outfits and hats, but also looking after Her Majesty's health and well-being, and communicating with her team of expert professors and doctors.

As Curator, I would be responsible for The Queen's personal jewellery and certain pieces from the Crown Jewels, as well as The Queen's Insignia. It is a great honour and privilege to be entrusted with the care of The Queen's private jewellery and to help select items that are worn on a daily basis.

One of the first things I wanted to do in this new role as Curator was to find a jeweller with whom I could build a relationship, as the previous Crown Jeweller was due to retire. They would oversee one of the rarest collections of gems and historical pieces, some of which have never been seen, and would need to be extremely knowledgeable about the repair and restoration of antique jewellery. And, as is the case with all staff members in the Royal Household, they would need to be very discreet.

Having discussed this idea with Her Majesty, who agreed, I knew exactly where to begin my search; the Royal Palace itself, which often proved to be a fountain of knowledge. Not wanting to rouse anyone's suspicions, I mentioned to several people that I was looking to commission a jeweller to design something for myself, and time and time again the same name was suggested: Mr Harry Collins from G. Collins & Sons, who was based in Royal Tunbridge Wells, Kent. Her Majesty often chooses smaller, family-run businesses to work with and was not in the slightest bit bothered by the fact that Mr Collins was based outside of London, so a date was soon set for him to come to Buckingham Palace and bring a selection of his work.

A week later, a very anxious Mr Collins arrived for his appointment, unaware that I had arranged for Her Majesty to join us. Shortly before The Queen's

Opposite: *The symbolic 'Girls of Great Britain and Ireland' Tiara is one of my favourite pieces.*

arrival, I asked him to display his silverware on the table and wait outside the room. Understandably, Harry seemed a little unnerved as he left. Her Majesty joined me to review his work and she was keen to purchase a few salvers and trinkets, so I proceeded to go and bring Mr Collins back into the room. I had to put him under pressure to see how he would cope, especially if I gave him a particular piece of jewellery from The Queen's collection. I needed to be sure that he would be able to work under stress if necessary.

I always find it fascinating to see how differently people respond on first meeting The Queen. Unsurprisingly, Mr Collins was rather taken aback, and after the formal introductions, he began to discuss his work with Her Majesty, going into detail about his style and techniques. The Queen kept glancing in my direction and I knew from the look on her face that she was happy – this was her seal of approval and a signal to present Mr Collins with a beautiful leather fitted case which contained the Vladimir Tiara.

I brought the case in and placed it on the table. Then I opened the box and took out the tiara, handing it to Mr Collins and explaining what was needed. Mr Collins delicately took the tiara from me and held it as gently as one would hold a baby. Carefully turning the headpiece to examine its diamonds and pear-shaped, cabochon-cut emeralds, he was clearly transfixed and I noticed that he kept staring at the tiara and Her Majesty in turn. It struck me that he was frozen to the spot – still smiling, but saying no words: it was as though he had stage fright. Luckily, The Queen is very adept in these situations and simply flashed Mr Collins a huge smile which helped snap him out of his trance.

'Mr Collins,' Her Majesty said calmly, 'do you think you would be able to alter the casting on the drops of the emeralds?' Harry agreed, so I asked how much the re-casting would cost. 'Not much,' was his response, so I asked again. Once again, his response was vague and he looked nervously towards Her Majesty, only for her to say, 'Don't look at me, Angela does the money'. Putting Mr Collins under pressure, I asked one final time, 'Please can you give me an estimate, Mr Collins?' and he finally quoted a price which was agreeable to everyone.

Mr Collins has been an integral part of our team over the years and in June 2000, The Queen had a special request for him – to design a special piece of jewellery for her mother, Queen Elizabeth, to mark her 100th birthday. Needless to say, he was thrilled to be asked, and when Mr Collins returned a couple of weeks later to discuss some ongoing restoration work, he told Her Majesty that he had, 'come up with a lovely idea for your mum's present', producing a superbly designed brooch. It was a very unusual piece, handmade in 18-carat

'Don't look at me, Angela does the money.'

Opposite: *The Vladimir Tiara is made up of fifteen intertwined diamond-set ovals from which hang pendant pearls. The pearls can be interchanged with emeralds.*

gold with a cabochon-cut centre of rock crystal and featuring a painstakingly fine hand-painted centenary rose set among 100 diamonds, to give the appearance that it is floating.

The Queen was delighted. When I escorted Mr Collins out of the Palace that day, I thought it was important to point out that although it wasn't a major issue, it was more correct to refer to members of the Royal Family by their full title, rather than 'mum'. Mortified, he asked me to pass on his apologies and even informed me later that the next day he'd purchased a copy of the Debrett's book on etiquette.

A few weeks later, the day came to present Her Majesty with the brooch, and upon his arrival, it was clear that Mr Collins had been carefully studying how one should supposedly behave around The Queen. He greeted Her Majesty and presented her with the magnificent fitted case in which the brooch sat and, having read somewhere that where possible, one should not turn their back on The Queen, he proceeded to walk away backwards. Unfortunately, Mr Collins failed to notice Linnet, one of Her Majesty's corgis, lying on the floor behind him. He tripped over Linnet and ended up next to the dog, lying spread-eagled on the carpet. Terrified that he'd hurt one of The Queen's dogs, Harry frantically rubbed Linnet's chest, apologising profusely, but Her Majesty reassured Mr Collins and told him not to worry: it was not his fault as the corgis had a terrible habit of lying in the most awkward places.

From that point on, Mr Collins and I formed a fruitful working relationship which saw him tend to some of the most significant pieces in Her Majesty's collection, including the alteration of the Vladimir Tiara and of the Countess of Wessex's wedding tiara, which was recently redesigned for the State Banquet with President Trump. Mr Collins is truly an invaluable member of the team.

I have also had the privilege to work with various other jewellers, Swarovski Crystals and Mappin & Webb to name just a couple. The fourth of June 2013 was to be the sixtieth anniversary of Her Majesty's Coronation and Mark Appleby, from Mappin & Webb, called me explaining that the company wanted to design a brooch to give to The Queen in honour of this special occasion. Mark and I discussed the idea and it was agreed that it should be an orchid brooch made from Waterford Crystal. I particularly liked the idea of using the crystal, as you would then be able to see the colour of The Queen's outfit through it. The brooch consisted of four hand-cut Waterford Crystal orchid flowers surrounded by sixty-six diamonds, which would be attached to rose gold stamens. The brooch was lovely and Her Majesty wore it during the Irish State Visit at Windsor Castle, which was particularly fitting as Waterford Crystal is based in Ireland.

Above: *The Queen's special handmade birthday gift for The Queen Mother.*

Opposite: *The pearls for the Vladimir Tiara are kept in numbered pouches and it can take nearly an hour to change them.*

MY PRETTY
WOMAN MOMENT

By the year 2001, I had begun designing outfits for The Queen and I wanted to ensure that from then on Her Majesty always looked her best and was up-to-date on the latest trends. As part of my role as a designer, I was responsible for searching for another designer whose creations might be suitable for The Queen, as I knew I wouldn't be able to do it all myself. Usually this is an enjoyable task, but on one occasion, things didn't go as smoothly as I'd hoped.

On one of my first solo excursions, I was planning to visit some local designers, not far from Buckingham Palace. I dressed in smart-casual clothes, but comfortably, as anyone might do when they're anticipating a morning of walking around the shops. The first shop I went into had a stale feel to it and the outfits in the window display seemed slightly old-fashioned. None the less, I was approached by a lady who smiled and asked if she could help. I explained that I'd come to have a look at their clothes and asked whether I could see the clothes on the rails to gain a better idea of the style and cut of their designs, as well as the finishing. As she agreed, I spotted a man at the back of the room who, even though he was in the middle of fitting someone, was staring at me as if I was the dirt on his shoe. He peered over the top of his black-rimmed glasses and condescendingly advised that the clothing was 'couture, not retail'.

I was shocked by his rudeness and immediately turned to the woman who had greeted me and I said quietly, 'I do know it's couture, not retail, thank you. And he has just made a big mistake. Huge. I will be back to tell him who he missed designing for.' In my mind I was Julia Roberts in *Pretty Woman* right then!

With that, I left the shop feeling humiliated and belittled. How rude of him to presume my status in such a way.

I made my way to the next shop, hoping for a more positive experience. I had been recommended to try Motcomb Street by one of The Queen's Ladies-in-Waiting as a good area to find designers, so I went into Stewart Parvin Couture. As I stepped inside, it felt different from the last place – bright and modern with beautiful outfits everywhere. Again, a lady met me with a beaming smile and I asked the same questions as before: whether they'd mind me looking at the designs, the cut and the finishing of their clothes. 'Not at all, take your time,' was the very different response, and I went along the rails freely, looking at all the outfits. It was immediately clear to me that this was not only the work of a designer but of an excellent tailor. I was so impressed that I asked if it would be possible to meet Mr Parvin and, sure enough, the lady offered me a seat while she went to fetch him.

I had to wait only ten minutes for Mr Parvin, during which time I kept looking towards a particular blue cocktail outfit with the most lovely harlequin multi-coloured gem buttons. In fact, I was engrossed in these buttons when a young man in a pair of jeans and a white T-shirt greeted me warmly and enthusiastically. I explained to Stewart (for that was who he was) that, having looked at his designs, I had my eye on the blue cocktail suit with diamanté buttons, but that I would need to take the piece away for a short while to show my employer. I promised to bring it back within a few hours. Bear in mind that, at this point, Stewart had no idea who I was or for whom I worked, but he agreed: he really was the warm, friendly person he appeared to be.

Two hours later, I returned with the outfit, which I had shown to The Queen and had received her approval on Stewart's style. Stewart was there to greet me again and, after thanking him, I asked if he had a stockroom. Sure enough, he took me straight downstairs to show me, seemingly unfazed by my endless questions about his work. Three of his materials leaped out at me as being appropriate for Her Majesty – a blue fleck tweed among them. With these in mind, I asked Stewart if he would do some quick designs there and then for a very high-profile female customer. Once again, Stewart was happy to oblige and we spent some time sketching potential designs. Safe in the knowledge that Stewart was a talented, trustworthy, and kind person, I finally disclosed that these designs would be for Her Majesty The Queen, but that he must be discreet and keep everything confidential.

And that was that. Since then, Stewart and I have been working together for The Queen, and our friendship and professional relationship have gone from strength to strength. Sometimes it's hard to believe that we have known each other for over eighteen years. In 2007, Stewart was granted his Royal Warrant in recognition of his contribution to The Queen's wardrobe. Little does that first designer know what he missed out on.

This was not only the work of a designer but of an excellent tailor.

Happy times – Stewart and I collaborating together at Joel & Son. Look out for this material used in a cocktail dress to be worn in 2020.

ALL IN A DAY'S WORK

As my role evolved and became even more varied, I soon learned that there would be no 'typical' day for me, just as there is no 'typical' day in Her Majesty's schedule, with its various engagements, Royal Tours and State Visits.

A couple of years ago, in 2017, a request from the Castle Administrator at Glamis Castle, Tommy Baxter, made its way to my desk in a handwritten letter from Angus, Scotland. Tommy was looking to organise an exhibition to mark the eightieth anniversary of King George VI's Coronation and was wondering if The Queen would be willing to loan The Queen Mother's wedding dress, her Coronation dress and Coronation robe for display, as well as the Coronation dresses, robes and coronets of Their Royal Highnesses The Princess Elizabeth and The Princess Margaret. Tommy mentioned that he thought it was unlikely: he had already been in touch with a member of the Royal Household and been offered two paintings for the exhibition, but no outfits.

Glamis Castle is very close to The Queen's heart as it is where her mother, Queen Elizabeth, grew up and where Her Majesty was often taken as a child, with her sister, Princess Margaret. I knew that The Queen had wonderful memories of the historic castle, so I decided to ask whether we could agree to Tommy's request. Her Majesty was happy to do so, and asked me to 'help them as much as you can', even noting that some of those items had recently been on display in Buckingham Palace – there seemed no reason why they could not be loaned for the exhibition in Glamis Castle. Tommy was thrilled when I told him, but gaining The Queen's approval turned out to be the easiest part of this process.

After much correspondence, my personal assistant, Jackie Newbold, and I found a suitable date to deliver everything to Glamis. We had to consider transport carefully – the cases must never be out of sight – so we decided that the train would be our safest option. With a case each – one containing the Princesses' small dresses, robes and coronets, the other with The Queen Mother's dress and robe – we made our way, alone and with no security, for a two-night stay in Dundee. God help anyone who tried to take the cases from us that day! We weren't stressed: we were alert, very aware, and very watchful.

Opposite: Jackie and I working hard.

The Queen Mother's robe, worn during King George VI's Coronation. Regal at its best.

When we arrived at the Castle, we got straight to work. When it comes to any exhibition or display of The Queen's things, I tend to have a lot of input, so that Her Majesty is safe in the knowledge that everything will be displayed or showcased in just the right way. Jackie and I were thrilled to help the Earl of Strathmore and the Dowager Countess make a truly breathtaking exhibition.

Before we headed back to London, I was reminded that The Queen was in need of some checked skirts, so Doreen, one of Tommy's colleagues, was kind enough to take us to the Fabric Mill at Halley Stevensons – the perfect place to find something suitable for Her Majesty. All in all, it was a very fruitful trip.

The exhibition ran for five months and Tommy regularly emailed with updates to say how well it was going and how much the public enjoyed seeing the Coronation outfits. During our stay in Balmoral that year, The Queen herself went to Glamis Castle to have a look at her mother's dress and robe, and her younger sister's outfit, on display in that beautiful setting. It must have brought back such fond memories.

As the exhibition came to a close, Jackie and I arranged a date to collect the outfits. It was a particularly busy time of year so we decided to travel up to Dundee and come back immediately – everyone thought we were crazy for not staying overnight, even The Queen. But when the diary is that full, you do what you have to do. On the day, we had only a fifteen-minute window in which Tommy was to meet us on the station platform to return the cases and, as luck would have it, the train was running five minutes late. Needless to say, Jackie and I were slightly on edge. Happily, the exchange went smoothly (and very quickly!) and we were immediately on our way back to London with the priceless cargo. All in a day's work!

'Help them as much as you can'

CHAPTER 2

Our Working Year

DESIGNING FOR THE QUEEN

The Queen accepts more than 300 engagements each year, through different seasons, occasions, and cultures. Our role as her dressers is to ensure that Her Majesty is appropriately attired for each occasion – from State events to informal daywear, in the United Kingdom and abroad.

From time to time The Queen will wear the same outfit to different events, although several months will pass between them. When I'm designing an outfit, I start with 'feelers': large samples of material that allow me to experience the texture of the fabric before deciding to buy it. I will squeeze and twist the sample in my hands, before smoothing it out again. If the material remains crumpled or creased, it will be of no use and is discarded from the selection.

I get my inspiration from seeing and touching the materials too, rather than starting with a sketch. I find a quiet moment when I hide in the materials storeroom and play with the fabrics, allowing them to shape themselves into a design. I look for movement with soft, light materials, and might even switch on a fan to see how they behave in a breeze. Fabric choices are obviously important – there are beautiful fabrics that work well but might catch or pull on objects like Her Majesty's watch. Loose-weave fabrics can easily lose their shape, requiring a good lining to prevent this. They can also develop loose strands, making them appear unkempt and unattractive.

Colour is key, though – the colour chosen must suit The Queen and the occasion. Vibrant colours work well in the daytime: they allow her to stand out from the crowd and be visible to the well-wishers who have come to see her. As the light changes, or when Her Majesty moves to an interior space, this will have an effect on the colour and texture of the fabric, and this must be taken into account.

I consider the four seasons separately and individually when designing for The Queen. Spring is for delicate, paler colours, flower motifs, lightweight coats and jackets, but as the weather is changeable, I must ensure that warmer fabrics are used to shield Her Majesty from the chill. Summer is for light, dynamic

Previous page: The Queen at Royal Ascot in 2019.

Opposite: *My design room at Buckingham Palace. This outfit was worn during the Diamond Jubilee concert at Buckingham Palace and demonstrates how well The Queen and I work together. I designed the outfit with the detailing on the left shoulder, and The Queen requested it on her right shoulder, which is exactly how she wore it on the night.*

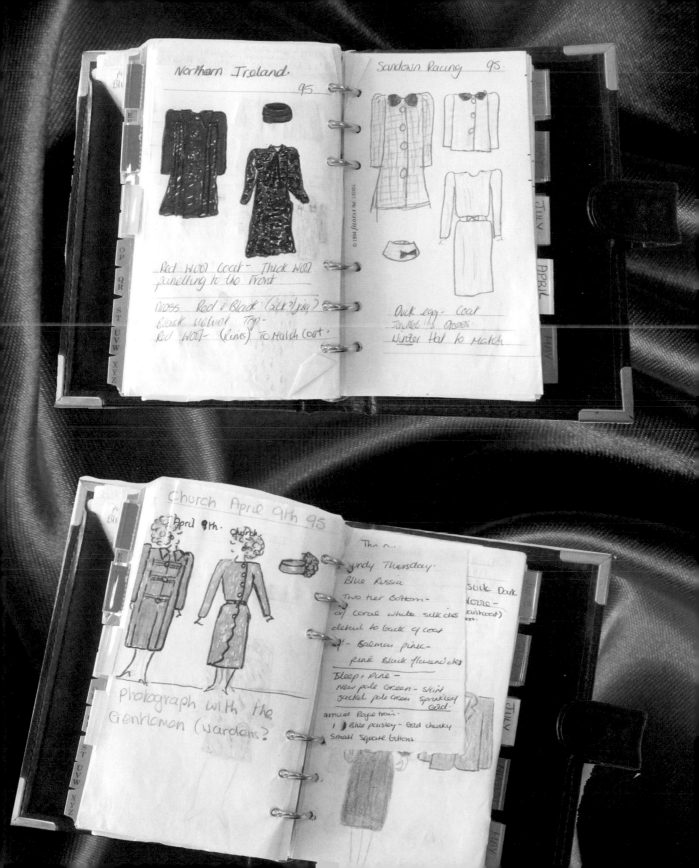

I choose mainly striking colours so that The Queen will be easily seen.

fabrics that move and flow with the breeze; strong florals work, with vibrant colours. Autumn is cooler, and I introduce medium to heavier fabrics, such as wools, cashmere and double crêpes, with a mellower colour palette. Winter brings gold, royal blue, deep purple, as well as velvets and heavier wools, with matching scarves, larger collars and warm hats. If Her Majesty is due to attend an engagement in particularly cold weather, from 2019 onwards fake fur will be used to make sure she stays warm.

Although there are, of course, many beautiful garments and outfits, there is also the casual side to Her Majesty, when she goes walking with her dogs, for example. Although The Queen is famous for her green macs and her Wellington boots, The Queen also likes to wear skirts and blouses. The Queen has a mixture of silk blouses as well as cotton shirts, which are all handmade by Grosvenor Shirts Ltd in Jermyn Street. As you can imagine, over the years The Queen now has many blouses and shirts, but she also wears cotton dresses in hot weather. And this is where Karl Dunkley and Juan Credidio at Grosvenor Shirts really come into their own, making these more casual outfits in their factory in Ireland.

Many of The Queen's more memorable dresses are created for specific events, such as a State ceremony or a Royal Tour abroad. When a tour is in prospect, The Queen will review the designs with me to find a style that will be sympathetic to the people and culture of the country she is to visit.

In general, necklines on coats and jackets must not be too high or too low, and must not restrict The Queen's movement. This is particularly true of thick wool coats with wide, full collars. A low neckline on a long dress allows a distinctive necklace to sit well and to be seen. In warmer weather I typically design with a more open neckline, and when cooler the neckline will be higher and closed for warmth and comfort.

When Her Majesty is travelling in a car and sitting for long periods, her coat or jacket must be comfortable and practical, and she must be confident on getting out of a vehicle that her outfit will fall correctly and not crumple. Too much fabric can prove challenging in that situation – and large, heavy beading on a gown can be uncomfortable, especially on the back or when sitting down. None the less, The Queen understands that beading and crystals are sometimes necessary to produce a spectacular effect: she doesn't mind temporary discomfort when it is so important for her to 'look the part'. I usually add a few extra layers of lining to help cushion the impact, especially at the back of the dress, and try to keep the heavily beaded areas to the front and sides.

The lengths of dresses vary according to the occasion: daywear will usually stop just below the knee; a cocktail dress for a drinks reception could fall to just below the knee again or ballerina length, finishing just on or below the bottom of the calf. This length is particularly good as it enables Her Majesty to walk

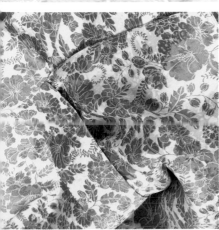

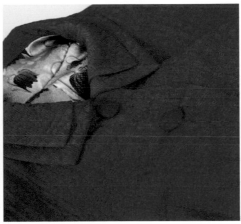

unhindered. Stairs can present a problem with dresses if they are too long or too tight. On occasion you will see The Queen wearing skirts that flare out from a fitted hip or knee as they allow for easy movement. I often use a fishtail in long skirts, as this gives a lovely shape to the back while still allowing for movement. Overall, The Queen likes her clothes to be fitted but not too tight, with a sleeve length of either three-quarters or full – definitely not too wide at the wrists: at lunch or dinner the cuffs might end up in the soup.

The 'EU dress' – see full story on page 137.

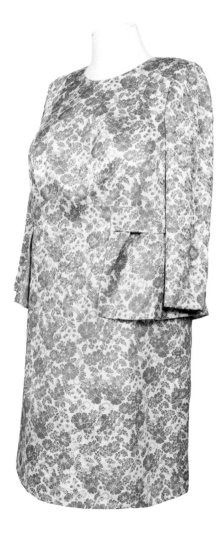

When the time comes, I arrange a meeting with The Queen to go through my design ideas, suggested outfits and material choices. It usually takes no longer than an hour, and once we've come to an agreement, the outfits are made swiftly. Two fittings are then arranged to ensure that each garment fits Her Majesty perfectly.

The Queen's shoes are mostly handmade – and usually with no more than a 2-inch heel, although for uneven surfaces, such as cobbles, gravel, or grass, she will wear shoes with a lower heel. In the mid-2000s I was looking to modernise Her Majesty's shoe collection, so I called in an expert, and friend, Michael Atmore, the Editorial Director of Fairchild Publications. Known in the industry as the 'Shoe Whisperer', he suggested that I reconnect with Rayne Shoes, under the new direction of Nick Rayne. Rayne Shoes had a long history of supplying the Royal Family, but had stopped doing so after a change in ownership and direction. After this successful re-introduction, Michael also introduced me to Stuart Weitzman, Neil Clifford at Kurt Geiger and Carvela and Manolo Blahnik. Her Majesty tends to use cream, white or black for her shoes as one pair will match, and be worn with, many different outfits. As has been reported a lot in the press, a 'flunky' wears in Her Majesty's shoes to ensure that they are comfortable and that she is always good to go. And yes, I am that 'flunky'. The Queen has very little time to herself, and no time to wear in her own shoes, and as we share the same shoe size it makes the most sense this way.

Like The Queen's shoes, most of her handbags are custom made, and weight is very important – given that Her Majesty may have to carry it for some time. She prefers a longer handle so that it hangs from her forearm without catching on the cuffs. The Queen doesn't have favourites, and uses handbags from different designers.

The Queen is conscious that she must be easily visible to as many people as possible when she is out and about so I choose mainly striking colours so that she will be easily seen. For example, when

A 'flunky' wears in Her Majesty's shoes to ensure that they are comfortable. And yes, I am that 'flunky'.

Her Majesty visits a school or a children's centre, she is always dressed in a bright, jolly colour, and her hat has the kind of details that will appeal to children – feathers, twirls, twists, flowers, and ribbons. When she visits a nursing or residential home for older people, she prefers to wear a strong, well-defined colour, with a structured hat, to help those who are visually impaired to see her and feel part of the visit. In fact, when The Queen's engagement includes a walkabout, the size of the crown and brim of the hat are also taken into account, as The Queen is aware that people travel from far and wide hoping to get a glimpse of her and it is important that young and old can see her clearly on the day. But the crown of the hat must not be so high that Her Majesty has difficulty with getting into and out of a vehicle. After 6pm, The Queen does not usually wear a hat, but on State occasions or when attending special dinners, she may wear a headpiece or a tiara to go with a beautiful evening dress.

If Her Majesty has to attend a large number of engagements in one day – sometimes up to five – I go for zips every time in her dresses: it is much more convenient for The Queen to be able to step in and out of a dress quickly: trying to lift a garment over the head can also wreak havoc with the hair. I also use discreet weights in the hemlines – many of The Queen's engagements take place in the open air where a sudden breeze can be troublesome.

Typically, the lifespan of an outfit can be up to around twenty-five years. Her Majesty is always thrifty and likes her clothes to be adapted and recycled as much as possible. Given how much attention is paid to what The Queen wears, the Assistant Dressers and I do take into consideration how regularly an outfit is worn. After two or three outings, a piece will have become familiar to the media and public, so we will either look for ways to modify it or it will become something that is worn on private holidays at Balmoral or Sandringham, or as a morning dress. Older outfits are handy considering that, just like all of us, Her Majesty is likely to encounter the odd muddy dog.

Dress worn in 2018.

THE QUEEN'S WARDROBE

There has been much speculation about the private rooms in Buckingham Palace, both in terms of their number and how they are used. However, Her Majesty is a very modest lady and only occupies a few rooms: her bedroom; her private sitting room; her dressing room and bathroom, and the Audience Room, which is where she meets with the Prime Minster and other dignitaries, and The Empire Room, which is a waiting room. These rooms aren't vast and there is space for very little furniture: just the odd wardrobe or chest of drawers.

Even after twenty-five years of service with Her Majesty, it still astonishes me that some former members of staff – even those who have not worked in the Palace for thirty years – are prone to making suggestions and sharing supposed details about The Queen's private rooms, when they actually have no insight whatsoever. The only gentlemen that I have ever known to enter these rooms are The Duke of Edinburgh and other members of the Royal Family, because The Queen's privacy is the absolute priority among her personal staff. So, do bear this in mind the next time you hear any supposed details about Her Majesty's private rooms! There will always be people who will say anything for attention.

Some former members of staff are prone to sharing supposed details about The Queen's private rooms when they actually have no insight whatsoever.

Opposite: *Part of The Queen's private wardrobe.*

Like any woman, The Queen is very practical and has her everyday items accessible to her, such as day dresses, hanging in the wardrobe in her dressing room which are ready to wear. Outfits that Her Majesty would wear on special occasions or for outside engagements are kept in a wardrobe upstairs, along with longer evening gowns, so that whenever The Queen wishes to see these items, she can pop upstairs to browse through them. Having the upstairs space is equally as convenient for me, as when I am preparing for an upcoming Royal Tour, it would be impractical to try to safely move all of the many outfits and their matching hats to her dressing room to go through. Instead, selections are made based on sketches and material samples which I show to Her Majesty, and all the designing and creation of the outfits takes place on the Dressers' Floor.

Part of my varied role involves looking after these personal rooms, along with Her Majesty's two Pages. With the help of the Assistant Dressers, I ensure that Her Majesty's wardrobe is properly organised and ready for the day ahead and The Queen's Housemaids will clean all her rooms daily. I am always respectful of Her Majesty's privacy and we try to make sure that she has a little time to herself.

Below left: *Calling bells originated during Queen Victoria's reign, when wiring was first put into Buckingham Palace. These are the same ones still used today to signal us from Her Majesty's private rooms.*

Below right and opposite: *Part of The Queen's private wardrobe.*

THE TEAM

Our team is like a wedding cake. On the top tier is Her Majesty, of course, followed by me underneath. Then we have the Deputy Dresser, Timea, followed by three Assistant Dressers – Grace, Phoebe and Lucy – who assist me with The Queen's wardrobe. The title 'Dresser' could be a bit misleading as Her Majesty actually dresses herself. Our role is to lay everything out for her and sometimes help zip her up or fasten a tricky piece of jewellery, although The Queen doesn't need help with her everyday jewellery such as her pearls and earrings.

After the Assistant Dressers is Jackie, my Personal Assistant. She not only looks after the work side of things – managing my diary, organising meetings, the bills – but also me personally, helping me get to the places I need to be at on time as my day can be quite hectic. With Jackie there, I know everything will be in order.

Next is Neil, who is our Project Manager and who runs the floor. Anything to do with maintenance or the removal of luggage – whether it is a large number of cases to be sent to Windsor or Balmoral, or smaller, everyday deliveries – Neil deals with other members of the Royal staff to make sure everything is organised. He is also helpful when it comes to setting up meetings with property services and the travel office and making sure everything is organised.

Then we have Stella, who is our milliner. Stella makes Her Majesty's hats based on my designs and I often ask for her input on which trimmings work best together – I really value her ideas and suggestions.

We also have a dressmaker, Desiree, who makes the clothes once I have designed them and they have been approved by Her Majesty. As with Stella, the dressmaker will suggest alterations and additions and she always knows exactly how I am picturing an outfit. I'll often say, 'Yes, that's it – that's exactly what I want!' She works on it from the very start to the finish, from cutting the pattern all the way to the completed article.

Finally, we have a housemaid who focuses specifically on the Dressers' Floor and helps to keep things organised and tidy. She will assist with packing and labelling each item.

An important thing that helps to keep our team running like clockwork is that everyone is trained in each other's roles. Jackie, for example, is trained as an Assistant Dresser and Stella can make alterations and repairs to dresses. So,

Opposite: *The crème de la crème, in 2019.*

if I happen to be ill or on holiday, someone else can step in. Everyone covers everything and works together seamlessly.

However, I do have strict rules on the Dressers' Floor. Firstly, I don't hold with gossip or little spats between staff members. I run a happy ship and everyone needs to feel that we're a small family. Secondly, no one can come onto our floor without an invitation or not having made an appointment, because there could be private clothes out that we're in the process of washing or ironing. I think that if any of my team was asked what they think of me, they'd say I was fair. They know what I'd say about them – that they're the crème de la crème.

The title 'Dresser' could be a bit misleading as Her Majesty actually dresses herself.

2002
2002
2002
2002
A53
A51
2007
Banner
Banner
HOLYROOD
JUNE 2019
30 Sunday
A|T
Call
Lavender crêpe morning dress
Bfast
Stewart Parvin 'Peonies' A line coat in powder blue crêpe. Silk dress in shades of powder blue and pink. Hat by RTM. Sapphire + diamond grape brooch. Rubber soles. Left dress on for lunch. Changed the brooch to small diamond flower clip.
11:10 Church Canongate Kirk 12:15 Return
Lunch
Tea
No change
20:30 Dinner HM only
Change back into morning dress
HOLYROOD
2019 JULY
Monday 1
HAIR IAN
A|T
Call
Daisy print silk dress
Bfast
Lunch
No change
No change
16:15 Hair Ian
Angela Kelly 'Autumn Breeze' Cocktail dress in silk chiffon with turquoise/mocha/beige leaf prints. Patent toe shoes. Double aquamarine and diamond clips.
Lord Chamberlain's Reception
20:30 Dinner
No change
2005
2005
A51 APPT
A51 APPT
A51 APPT
A51 APPT
2006
2010
2010
2010
2011
2011

OUR
ANNUAL
DIARY

While it is impossible to predict what each year will bring, there are certain annual events and engagements that will forever remain unchanged.

The Christmas holiday season always starts in the middle of December at Sandringham House, in Norfolk, where Her Majesty is based until early February. After Christmas and New Year, which The Queen spends with her family, Her Majesty will invite private guests to Sandringham, who tend to stay until the beginning of February. Even throughout the Christmas period, The Queen will continue to work on her red boxes. Usually, Her Majesty will only return to Buckingham Palace after the anniversary of the death of her father, George VI, on 6 February. It's certainly a sad time for The Queen but I am sure that she finds comfort in the memories that Sandringham holds for her.

Upon returning to Buckingham Palace, Her Majesty's schedule resumes at full pace with a host of daily private audiences, weekly meetings with the Prime Minister and occasional meetings with the Privy Council, as well as the odd evening function. In the run-up to Easter, Her Majesty will hold several Investitures and will typically hold at least one State Visit before joining her family for the Easter weekend. The day before Good Friday, The Queen attends a Maundy service before heading into the Easter Court, which varies each year, depending on when the Easter weekend falls. One constant occasion is Her Majesty's birthday, which falls on 21 April and is celebrated privately with her family. Typically, Easter Court will finish towards the end of the month or at the beginning of May, when The Queen will travel to Wood Farm, a private cottage located on the Sandringham Estate.

May is always an exciting time of year from my perspective, as it is the start of the Garden Party season and Her Majesty can start to wear lighter fabrics and beautiful florals. As spring gets under way, The Queen hosts several garden parties, and the Windsor Horse Show takes place in the Home Park at Windsor. Perhaps the highlight of the season is the Chelsea Flower Show, which Her

*Opposite: **Our record keeping has definitely built up over the years!***

Majesty looks forward to every year, and after which she will always travel to Craigowan, a small private house on Balmoral Castle Estate.

The second of June sees Coronation Day, which Her Majesty marks privately before attending the Epsom Derby in Surrey. The next Royal engagement is a very well-known one: Trooping the Colour, a ceremony performed by regiments of the British and Commonwealth armies to mark the official birthday of the British Sovereign. It may be of interest to know that the reason Her Majesty has two birthdays is because her great-grandfather, King Edward VII, who was born in November, always found the weather at that time of year to be disagreeable for the soldiers and members of the public who came out to celebrate the occasion. He therefore decided to arrange an official birthday parade in June, called Trooping the Colour, as it was near enough guaranteed that the weather would be more pleasant. After this grand event, Garter Day and Royal Ascot are soon upon us.

As June comes to a close, Her Majesty will visit the Palace of Holyroodhouse, in Edinburgh, where she hosts her final Garden Party of the year before visiting Wood Farm, at Sandringham, again for a short stay. From hereon in, we exclusively focus on preparing for Her Majesty's stay at Balmoral Castle. We head up to Scotland in mid-July, firstly to Craigowan Lodge and then we move across to the Castle, and we will not return to London until early October. While at Balmoral, Her Majesty will host picnics, barbecues, dinners, and shooting parties for her family, friends, and private guests, as well as two Highland Ghillies' Balls.

We specifically name the outfits to ensure we recognise them precisely if Her Majesty chooses to wear them again.

JUNE 2019   HOLYROOD

30 Sunday
181–184   PAYE week 13

WEEK 26

A/T

0800 Call
0830

0900 Bfast   Lavender crêpe morning dress
0930

1000

1030

11.10 Church   Stewart Parvin 'Peonies' A-line
Canongate Kirk   coat in powder blue crêpe.
12.15 Return   Silk dress in shades of powder
1230   blue and pink. Hat by Roy...
1300 ...   Sapphire + diamond...

After a busy but enjoyable summer, October sees us arrive back in London to a very different climate. Normal service resumes as soon as we return to the Palace, and it's not long before Her Majesty is hosting audiences, Investitures and her second State Visit of the year. Before long, November is upon us which usually involves the State Opening of Parliament, and attendance at The Royal Variety Show. Her Majesty also attends the Royal Albert Hall for the Festival of Remembrance, followed by the Cenotaph the following morning. As for anyone else in the country, December is a busy month for us, and alongside all the usual duties, Her Majesty will always take time to give Christmas presents to her staff at Buckingham Palace. An event she particularly looks forward to attending is the carol service in the Royal Mews, and festivities continue when The Queen hosts a Christmas lunch for the entire Royal Family.

Before you know it, the end of the year is approaching fast and we are soon packing to return to Sandringham. During The Queen's final weekend in Windsor, the choir from Windsor Castle comes to sing Christmas carols at the Sovereign's Entrance, which is always a special moment – particularly if it happens to be snowing! The Queen gives Christmas presents to the Windsor staff over this weekend. At this point, our only other event to prepare for is the filming of Her Majesty's Christmas message.

So, that's our year. There will always be changes to the programme, though, as Her Majesty may need to attend special events such as memorial or commemoration services, the opening of institutions or changes of Government. However, unexpected events aren't always serious occasions as sometimes there will be a wedding or christening to attend. Her Majesty may also need to sit for new portraits and there is always an excuse to take a trip on the Royal Train. Whatever her schedule, Her Majesty always rounds off each week by heading to Windsor Castle to relax and she will always attend church every Sunday, no matter where she is in the country.

HOLYROOD

27

HAIR IAN

2019 JULY

Monday 1

A/T PAYE week 13

182–183

Canada Day (Canada)

Daisy print silk dress

GARTER DAY

Garter Day takes place every June at Windsor Castle. It falls on the Monday of Royal Ascot week. This occasion is full of pomp and circumstance, and the Knights Companion and Ladies Companion of the Most Noble Order of the Garter, dressed in their velvet mantles, plumed hats and insignia, are a stunning sight. The Queen's Garter Robe is made from a royal blue velvet, lined with white satin. A red velvet hood is worn over the right shoulder, and the plumed hat is made from black velvet trimmed with white feathers.

King Edward III founded the Order in 1348, and on Garter Day any new Knights and Ladies take their oath and attend an Investiture, or installation, hosted by The Queen. As well as some 'extra' Knights and Ladies, who are members of the Royal Family, there are twenty-four Knights and Ladies at any one time, and they have been chosen personally by The Sovereign in recognition of their public service. It is a lifetime honour and each individual is designated their own banner, which is hung in St George's Chapel, Windsor.

Garter Day falls in what is generally a very busy period in The Queen's diary, and especially for us, ensuring all the outfits are packed and ready in time for the luggage transport from Buckingham Palace to Windsor Castle. The week before Garter Day and Royal Ascot, the Dressers' Floor at Buckingham Palace is a scurry of rails of clothes trundling along the corridor. Just as I check all the State Robes, the Garter Robe is hung up in the workroom beforehand and I inspect every inch of it, looking for any spots or bruising – a shiny mark   on the velvet. If there is any bruising, I will gently brush it out. To clean the robe, I fill a bathtub with hot water so the bathroom gets steamy, then hang the robe carefully away from the water. The steam will enable the creases to drop out. This works with any velvet. I never touch velvet with water and never iron it: doing either would damage the material. Once I am happy that the robe is clean and crease-free and the ribbons have been ironed, I pack it into a hanging bag and have it ready to take to Windsor Castle, along with the Royal Ascot racing outfits. By this point I will have already done similar checks on the outfits Her Majesty will be wearing to Ascot, ensuring all the buttons and trimmings are secure by giving them a sharp tug.

Once the luggage has been transferred to Windsor Castle from Buckingham Palace, a few days before Garter Day, the first thing I do when I arrive is take the

I fill a bathtub with hot water, then hang the robe

Opposite: The Queen on Garter Day in 2008.

Garter Robe to the workroom. I lay a sheet on the floor to protect the robe from dirt and damage when I take it out of the bag, then hang it on the back of a door and let the bottom of the robe drape along the sheet. I use a padded hanger with extra layers so that the robe fits it perfectly. Hanging the robe like this helps air it and allows any further creases to drop out.

On the Sunday, the day before Garter Day, I will press the ribbons again to make sure the robe looks pristine, then convey the robe to The Queen's dressing room. The State Dress Her Majesty will be wearing beneath the robe is pressed and checked – in particular making sure that the zipper works. The dress will be elegant and full length, but it will be an older design: when The Queen walks along the pavement from the Castle to St George's Chapel, the material may be damaged as the dress may drag a little along the ground. I wouldn't want a new dress of The Queen's to be marked or the hem to snag. I always prepare two spare full-length State Dresses in case there is an emergency, such as a button falling off or a hem becoming unstitched.

On the day, the Assistant Dressers and I attend The Queen and prepare everything for the busy day ahead. When The Queen departs for breakfast, we bring a coat stand into the dressing room, lay the sheet on the floor and hang the robe on the stand where it is ready for Her Majesty, with the State Dress near by. I also lay out the Garter chain, which is called the Collar. This is made up of twenty-four enamelled roses encircled with a blue buckled garter bearing the motto 'HONI SOIT QUI MAL Y PENSE' ('Shame on him who thinks ill of it.') These are linked together with twenty-four 'double lovers' knots' in gold. The Collar is worn suspended from the shoulders by white satin bows. It was introduced by King Edward III in 1348 and is also worn at the State Opening of Parliament, along with the Lesser George, an oval of plain gold that encircles St George and the Dragon with a buckled Garter and motto, which is worn by recipients of the Garter.

It may interest you to know that the 'Garter George' is a representation of Saint George killing the Dragon, set in exquisite gold and enamels. Some of the Royal Georges are embellished with jewels. Originally, the Lesser George was worn around the neck suspended from a narrow ribbon of Garter blue. Although The Queen has recently permitted this practice again, in order for people wearing black tie to wear the insignia, the Lesser George is supposed to suspend from the Garter's Broad Riband or 4-inch wide (for men) sash in Garter blue corded silk which goes over the left shoulder to suspend the Lesser George on the right hip.

After breakfast, The Queen will attend meetings with the Private Secretary. Then the Assistant Dressers and I will help Her Majesty get ready. She will change into her State Dress and put on her jewellery, then make her way to the Waterloo Chamber, where she will join the other members of the Order of the Garter for lunch. Once lunch has finished, The Queen returns to her dressing room where we help her put on the Garter Robe, the hood, plumed hat, and the Collar over the State Dress. We will remove the jewellery that The Queen wore to lunch and put it away. It is difficult to wear a necklace with the robe, as the Collar has to hook together for the robe to be secure on The Queen's shoulders and the pressure of the hook on a necklace would be uncomfortable.

The Queen and I often speak silently using eye contact – here she is smiling at me and silently telling me, 'You got here quickly!' And I really had! I had only just finished dressing Her Majesty and I ran (in high heels, of course) to be able to see the procession.

Garter Day is steeped in tradition, and people come from all over the world to line the processional route and watch the Knights and Ladies walk to St George's Chapel for a short service, at which any new Knights are installed. For many years, The Queen walked from Windsor Castle to St George's Chapel, but more recently carriages have been used. Royal Members of the Order usually join the procession, including The Duke of Edinburgh, The Prince of Wales, The Princess Royal, The Duke of York, The Earl of Wessex and The Duke of Cambridge.

While The Queen is away at the service, I prepare her clothes and jewellery to be worn at dinner, and when she returns, I help her remove all of the regalia and the robe. Her Majesty will change into a skirt and blouse, then perhaps go for a walk with her dogs. This is only the beginning of what will be a very busy week. I then take the robe and the State Dress to the workroom at Windsor Castle, where I check the robe before I put it away, and also check and press the State Dress before it is returned to the wardrobe.

The beautifully plush Garter Day robe.

The plumed hat from both angles, in all its glory.

ROYAL ASCOT

Royal Ascot is one of the most anticipated Royal events of the year. The racecourse was founded by Queen Anne in 1871, and the horse-races officially became a Royal Week in 1911. Even some of the races are Royal-themed, such as the Windsor Castle Stakes and the King George V Stakes. It was in 1825 that the first Royal Procession took place, with King George IV leading the coaches. Of course, Her Majesty has quite a few of her own horses that have entered and won on a number of occasions. So, only in extreme circumstances would Her Majesty not attend, and it is one of those rare occasions on which The Queen can relax and enjoy one of her best-loved interests, often watching her own horses race. Royal Ascot takes place in June and is one of the busiest weeks of our year, and also one of the most secretive, due to an incident a few years ago that involved inappropriate betting on the colour of The Queen's hat. Designing something different for this special week has its challenges. It's all about the horse-racing – one or more of Her Majesty's horses may be running – so my designs have to be practical for The Queen to get into and out of cars and also the Royal Carriages.

I usually start to plan for Royal Ascot in March, keeping in mind that many other events have been arranged, such as Easter Court, when The Queen stays at Windsor Castle, and the Royal Windsor Horse Show in May. Joel & Son Fabrics, the London fabric shop, provides some of the most beautiful material that is used in The Queen's clothing. They sell fabrics from across the world to the wider public and this is the shop I use most often to source what I need. Over the years Her Majesty has received fabrics as gifts, as I mentioned earlier, sometimes with beading and sequins, and also exquisite silks. Some are saved for future use, but during my years with Her Majesty, I have been able to use several such gifts in my designs.

I buy material from other sources too: in 2018 I was on holiday in Sri Lanka with my family, still on the lookout for inspiring materials. The tour guide took our group to a shop called Silk Gardens Ltd. The ladies there were wearing their traditional dress and I was in my element: it was a wonderland of colour. I came across a lovely raw silk and bought a few metres in purple, aqua, and green, which were kindly shipped to London.

Opposite: The Queen attends Ladies Day at Royal Ascot in 2019.

The Queen loves a bargain

At Joel & Son Fabrics I see Dino, who has looked after me for many years. Expert that he is, he updates me on all the latest fashions and colours. He will show me special materials, which are of the highest quality, and also less expensive fabric that is just as beautiful and still of the highest quality. His colleague Linda helps me when I choose the buttons, in which she is an expert.

While I'm looking at fabrics, ideas for how to use them come to mind, but I don't think in detail until I have a piece of material on a stand and I begin to drape it into a style that will suit The Queen. While the samples are being cut, I always peep into the bargain basket. The Queen loves a bargain and sometimes I luck out with a piece of material that I can conjure into a dress for her.

When Dino has the samples ready, he parcels them up and sends them to Buckingham Palace. I prepare my suggestions for what I think would work, with three possibilities for each fabric.

Sometimes I arrange to meet Stewart Parvin at Joel's and we talk about what different designs we will each do for Ascot Week. We talk about the colours we're thinking of, so if he is going for blue, I might opt to use yellow to ensure we don't overlap. Even though we have our own design styles, which are completely different, we might share a collar design or button: our main goal is always, of course, to ensure that The Queen looks beautiful. Thanks to Stewart's advice and guidance I have become the designer that I am today. Thank you, Stewart.

The Queen and John Warren cheer on her horse Estimate at Royal Ascot in 2013.

I will have lots of ideas for styles and colours for spring and summer, but I must choose the right ones, so I next make an appointment to show Her Majesty the samples I've picked out for her approval. This is a busy time for The Queen, so I need to schedule this important meeting at a time when I know we won't be rushed or interrupted. I meet The Queen at the appointed time in her dressing room and we go through all the samples together. The Queen listens to my suggestions and also provides feedback from previous outfits: she might, for example, notice that a high collar risks rubbing against the skin if worn with a certain style of dress with a lower neckline. Once everything is agreed, I place my final order with Dino – enough of each material for a dress, possibly a jacket and coat, and an extra metre for the hat.

When the materials arrive, I lay them out and start work on the outfits straight away. I plan the style of each one in my mind and play with the material on the stand, draping it one way, then another. I do this on my own, while flitting in and out between my regular daily tasks. I never draw or sketch the design at this point: I unite the colours and shapes and plan it in my head. I also think about necklines, collars, and hats to match the outfits. I make a few sketches, then arrange another appointment with The Queen to show them to her and ask for her approval. The Queen trusts me with the designs but I like to seek her advice. Her Majesty chooses a colour, or suggests colours that will complement each other. I then produce a final design and, depending on its

Far left: *The smile that says it all. The Queen with the Gold Cup after Estimate won in 2013.*

Left: Ryan Moore rides Estimate to victory in 2013.

level of detail, it can take up to four weeks before we have something ready for a fitting with Her Majesty. At this time of the year, I usually make ten outfits in total, five of which are for Ascot. Two outfits are kept as backup and the remaining three are saved for upcoming garden parties or for Her Majesty's annual visit to the Palace of Holyroodhouse.

For Ascot the hats are even more important than the outfits. Ascot is famous for ladies' hats! These bring their own challenge. Once The Queen and I are satisfied with the main fabrics for the dresses and coats, I will go to see Stella in the millinery room at the Palace and look through all the millinery fabrics we have in stock. If we don't already have what is needed, Stella will order it. She handmakes – no easy task – most of the silk flowers, leaves or sculptural details, although sometimes we source silk flowers from a respected German company. There is a lot to think about for each hat as I like my designs to be different every time. Stella and I chat about the hats, and with my designs and her suggestions we create something beautiful. And we keep the betting shops busy with people betting on the colour of The Queen's hat each year!

When a hat and an outfit are finished, I put them together and double-check that I'm completely happy. There have been times during the making of the outfits and hats that I have changed my mind and altered them. I have to be 100 per cent sure they will suit and look perfect on The Queen.

I show The Queen each outfit, with its hat, for her final approval, three or four weeks before Ascot. I take rails of all the new clothes – Stewart Parvin's as well as mine – with the hats to The Queen's dressing room. In addition to the hats designed by me and made by Stella to go with my outfits, Rachel Trevor-Morgan will make the hats for most of Stewart Parvin's outfits. Here, Her Majesty and I will go through them for any final tweaks. The Queen will choose an outfit in which she feels she will stand out among the crowds of racegoers, who will also be in their best clothes.

Once The Queen has agreed, I return the rails to the Dressers' Floor and the outfits are packed and stored until we are ready to leave for Windsor, usually on the Thursday or Friday before Ascot Week begins, depending on The Queen's other engagements.

When I look back at all the outfits and hats I have designed, and the hats that Stella has made, one particular hat stands out for me. It is the one The Queen wore to the Royal Wedding of Prince William and Catherine Middleton, now Their Royal Highnesses The Duke and Duchess of Cambridge. Her Majesty chose the colour, sunshine yellow, three weeks beforehand. It was such a significant occasion that the whole outfit, designed under my Angela Kelly label, had to be spot on. To mimic the sun's rays, we cut the material for the coat

larger than was necessary to allow for pleats to be pinched in and the matching hat – a matador shape made of crêpe and sinamay – was trimmed with two handmade satin roses and leaves. It was perfect.

Royal Ascot Week is a lot of fun for everyone in my team. The Dressers' Floor is bubbling with excitement, with everyone hoping to catch a glimpse of Her Majesty's new outfits and hats. They are all sworn to secrecy, of course, to keep the element of surprise, so I don't worry if they do take a peek: I trust them not to let any cats out of the bag!

In Ascot Week, Windsor Castle is even busier than usual, as guests will be staying there. My team is on call for dressing duties; they help to prepare The Queen's clothes, ensuring each outfit is pressed, its hemline checked, its buttons secure, and that there are no pulls or snags. Between them there is much speculation about what colour The Queen will choose to wear on opening day. On Saturday The Queen goes riding, and will spend time with her other horses. On Sunday she attends church and has a quiet afternoon when she may take the corgis out for a walk before any guests arrive for dinner.

Monday is Garter Day, and Royal Ascot begins on Tuesday. The atmosphere at Windsor Castle is electric. Each morning I place four or five previously worn hats on a table in the workroom. They are different colours and styles, and are on display for a reason. Anyone who happens to pass the room will see those hats. They are not hidden behind a closed door and no secret is made of them. This will stop anyone catching sight of the hat Her Majesty actually intends to wear and, with inside knowledge, betting a vast amount of money on the correct colour of The Queen's hat for opening day at Royal Ascot. This is cheating, and unfair on everyone else. It happened once, which was why this system was devised. Luckily, that year, the bookies clocked that something wasn't right with the bet in question, which was over £2,000, and they put a stop to it. Unfortunately, this meant that all bets on that day were called off. So the person who thought they were being clever just ruined the fun for everyone else.

I was horrified when I learned about the incident from the paper the next morning. When Ascot Week had finished, I attended a meeting with the owner of Paddy Power at which we agreed that betting on the colour of The Queen's hat would be closed at a certain time to avoid any cheating, but allowed people to carry on guessing the colour of The Queen's hat and perhaps even win a bit of money.

Every day in Ascot Week starts with The Queen dressing in her morning clothes. After breakfast, Her Majesty will call for each of her Private Secretaries, one by one. After her meetings with them, she returns to her dressing room. Three outfits are hanging on the clothes rail waiting for her, the hats placed on a table near by.

Just before lunch The Queen will choose from the three outfits. Even though the outfits for the opening day, Ladies Day and the final day have been selected, she will still have the two backup outfits to choose from in case she changes her mind. The final choice is made at the last minute but, believe me, that's still no guarantee, as the weather could change, which means the chosen outfit may not be suitable. Before she makes her final decision, The Queen consults the weather forecast to help her determine which outfit she will wear. Her Majesty would not usually wear a new outfit if it is raining as we would not know how the fabric will react to rain – it may shrink or crease – and instead may choose something she has worn before. If it is a clear, dry day, The Queen will wear a new outfit. If it is raining, she will use one of the many transparent umbrellas she has (each with a different-coloured trim to match any particular outfit she wears), which ensures that, even in the wettest conditions, she remains as visible as possible.

When The Queen chooses her outfit for the day, she will change into the dress for lunch, then go to join her guests in the private rooms of Windsor Castle. Lunch is very quick so that everyone can be ready to leave for the racecourse on time. When The Queen returns after lunch, she fixes her lipstick, adds a bit more blusher, puts on her hat, and secures it with hat pins. Finally, Her Majesty puts on her coat, picks up her gloves and handbag, gives us all a smile, and then she's off!

Right: *Bring on the rain, and the rainbow! The Queen has a clear umbrella with coloured trim that matches every outfit in case of rain – so she can still be seen.*

Opposite: *The blue hat is the 'EU hat' – now changed to a bow instead of the little flowers. See page 137 for the full story.*

There is no waiting around and certainly no fuss, as everything is done within three minutes, maybe four at the most. The Queen departs from the front door and leaves in the car that will drive her halfway to the racecourse. Then Her Majesty and her guests get out of the cars and step into the Royal Carriages, which will take them to the racecourse and on to the Royal Enclosure. It is much quicker by car to reach the halfway point to the racecourse, and The Queen and her guests' carriages need to follow a strict arrival schedule: each race starts at a specific time.

Once The Queen has left for the races, I contact the Palace Press Office in London and provide them with the much-anticipated information on what Her Majesty has chosen to wear that day. This will cover all the details of The Queen's outfit, including the colour, material, and the style of each piece and the hat. These details are immediately passed to the fashion commentators at the racecourse so that the radio and television presenters can announce it as Her Majesty is entering the racecourse arrival. This is also the moment when those who placed a bet on the colour of The Queen's hat find out if they have won!

My team and I always watch Royal Ascot on the television in my office and we all admire The Queen's and the other ladies' and gentlemen's attire, and take inspiration from the designs and colours on show. We listen to feedback on The Queen's outfit and hat, and I take pride in our work. You can see, even on the television, Her Majesty's passion and excitement and, of course, the thrill of the race.

When The Queen returns from racing, and depending on how comfortable she feels, she may keep on the same dress or change into something different. Eventually, the outfit she wore for Royal Ascot will be taken upstairs to be checked, pressed and hung in the wardrobe in the workroom. The hat is wrapped in tissue for protection and stored away. She will wear the outfit and hat once more later that year or the following year for another engagement.

With the day of racing over, it is time for the guests to retire to their rooms in Windsor Castle for a rest before dinner. In the meantime, the team and I will choose a dress for The Queen, and I will get out the jewellery for another night of sparkles.

The following day we start all over again – for the races and the evening dinner, the outfits for those occasions. Everything during Royal Ascot Week is orchestrated and timed so that it all runs smoothly for Her Majesty The Queen. I love it!

The Queen at Royal Ascot in 2019. When I saw The Queen on TV wearing this hat, I realised that the feathers were now dangling down too far on the right-hand side after travelling to the racecourse. I knew that would annoy The Queen, so I sent an urgent message to the Equerry to ask him to trim them down slightly, so they didn't come below the brim. However, the only scissors they could find at this short notice were enormous, so The Queen told him it would be fine to wait until she was back at Windsor Castle again. As soon as they returned later that day I was able to trim them properly with the right (sized!) equipment.

FOREVER THRIFTY

Sometimes, the special details that can take an outfit to another level are found in the most unexpected places. And often, they're the most inexpensive parts of an outfit.

In 2017, preparations for one of The Queen's Ascot outfits was going well. I had found some beautiful silk in the back of the stockroom with an eye-catching cerise floral pattern over an antique-gold background. I spend a lot of time in the stockroom, as new engagements come up often: in there I can plan and play with ideas. I thought initially that the flowers on that fabric were tulips but I soon learned that they were in fact called snake's-head fritillary – I'm always learning new things on the job. I was aware that Her Majesty had many outfits in cerise but decided it would be the best colour for the dress's accompanying coat and hat, as gold would not be appropriate for attending the races. Also, I knew that she would find a gold coat a little gaudy on this daytime occasion: it would appear too opulent.

With Ascot approaching, my team were making good progress with Her Majesty's outfit: the dress and coat were almost complete. However, although the hat from Stella was well under way, we had yet to decide on its trimmings. I had been pondering this for a few days, as I often do with more challenging designs – I'll often sleep on them and I find that an answer will present itself. I'd originally thought we could cut some of the fritillaries from the silk fabric to appliqué onto the hat, but had decided that this wasn't exciting enough for Ascot. I went looking for Paul Whybrew, The Queen's Page, for a solution. I found him in Her Majesty's storeroom, where something immediately caught my eye. In a corner, a modest plant pot contained snake's-head fritillaries in exactly the same cerise shade as The Queen's Ascot outfit! I couldn't believe it. Luckily for Stella and me, the fritillaries were made of silk, so once they had been well dusted, they could immediately be applied to Her Majesty's hat. A small detail such as this can really bring an outfit together. When I go shopping or out with family and friends to garden centres or department stores, I always visit the artificial flowers section in search of inspiration for the seasons ahead. It's always worth keeping your eyes open, as you never know where or when you might come across something useful!

Worn in 2019 – these silk flowers were a useful discovery!

THE PALACE OF HOLYROODHOUSE

The Palace of Holyroodhouse is The Queen's official Royal Residence in Edinburgh, and each year at the beginning of July, just after Royal Ascot, Her Majesty will spend a week there hosting and attending many different engagements, depending on her programme. The Royal Household staff who travel to Holyrood always look forward to this week. To be able to say that you are staying in the palace where Mary Queen of Scots once lived – how fabulous is that? Edinburgh is a fascinating and beautiful city, and when the staff have a bit of downtime, they venture in for a couple of hours. The Royal Yacht *Britannia* is docked there and some of the Royal Household staff worked on it many years ago. They like to visit it and reminisce about the happy times they spent aboard.

The run-up to Holyrood week is another busy time for us on the Dressers' Floor. I give The Queen a selection of sketches to choose from that includes outfits for the Garden Party she holds there and the official engagements she will attend and host. For a week's stay, there can be up to twelve outfits. The sketches include evening dresses for dinners.

Once the sketches have been approved and the outfits made, I oversee their packing, checking each item as it is placed in a hanging bag, and then I review the matching hats, making sure that the trimmings are attached properly before my team packs them carefully into hat boxes. They also pack clothing for everyday wear – skirts and blouses or perhaps a silk day dress. Finally, I pack the jewellery that Her Majesty will wear with each evening dress, as well as appropriate brooches for the day outfits.

Every other year, there is one more important item that must be packed: the Thistle Robe, to be worn by Her Majesty at the meeting of the Ancient and Most Noble Order of the Thistle. The Order was established in 1687 by King James VII of Scotland, who was also James II of England. Membership, which is lifelong, is the highest honour a person can receive in Scotland, and, like the Order of the Garter, it is given personally by The Queen at an installation ceremony. There are just sixteen Knights and Ladies in the Order at one time, with 'extra' Knights who are members of the Royal Family. The Knights and Ladies are men and women

Opposite: The Queen attends the Mass for the Order of the Thistle. Note that The Queen doesn't wear a necklace due to the cord which holds the robe together near the neck.

who have held public office or have made a significant impact on Scottish society.

The United Kingdom is famous for its ceremonies and traditions, especially when they involve the Royal Family. Some date back hundreds of years and the sight of Edinburgh's Royal Mile lined with people from all over the world watching the grand procession of the Knights of the Order of the Thistle is not to be missed.

The Thistle Robe is made of dark green velvet, lined with white satin and decorated with the Scottish insignia. It is worn with a white feather-plumed hat. On the robe a star shows the cross of St Andrew, with a green thistle in the centre on a field of gold. The collar is decorated with thistles and sprigs of rue. The pendant is of St Andrew and his cross and is reversible. One side shows St George and the Dragon (worn on Garter Day) and the other side is St Andrew for this service.

I pack two white State Dresses, one to be worn under the robe, with white gloves, silver shoes, and a matching silver handbag. I make the same preparations with the Thistle Robe as I do with the Garter Robe. I check to make sure the velvet has not been damaged and press the satin ribbons to make sure all the creases are out, then pack it into a hanging bag, ready for transport.

When Her Majesty arrives at the Palace of Holyroodhouse, a small ceremony takes place on the forecourt: the Presentation of the Keys. The Lord Provost, who is in charge of the city of Edinburgh, welcomes Her Majesty and offers her the keys to the city. The Queen accepts them, then immediately hands them back to the Lord Provost so that he can keep them safely for her next visit. During this ceremony, The Queen will inspect the Guard of Honour and the band will play the National Anthem, marking the official start to Holyrood week. For this event Her Majesty wears a smart day outfit – so, a beautiful dress, coat, and hat would be chosen.

While all this is happening outside, there is a scurry of activity inside The Queen's rooms as the Assistant Dresser and I unpack The Queen's luggage, making sure everything is in order as the week ahead will be extremely busy – and also highly enjoyable.

While at Holyrood, The Queen hosts a Garden Party to which as many as 8,000 guests will be invited. We always keep everything crossed for dry weather as everyone has to fit into the garden. The Queen will also hold an Investiture, audiences, or one-to-one meetings. The Queen will still meet with her Private Secretary and continue to work through her red boxes. Wardrobe changes come into play again, with between three and five every day: I have to make sure there are appropriate outfits available for each occasion for The Queen to choose from.

When it comes to the service for the Order of the Thistle, the Knights and Ladies begin their grand procession in the Signet Library, with music played by the Band of the Royal Regiment of Scotland. The group makes its way to the Chapel of the Order of the Thistle where Her Majesty will install any new members of the Order. Afterwards the Knights and Ladies walk to the Thistle Chapel in St Giles Cathedral where the ceremony will continue. Later on, The Queen hosts a small reception back in the Signet Library, one of Edinburgh's most splendid Georgian houses, which is followed by a lunch at Holyroodhouse.

This event used to take place at the beginning of our visit to Holyrood, but it has now been moved to near the end of the trip, which means that my team and I have to pack the robe and insignia, along with the rest of the luggage in a very short time, so that we leave punctually for either Wood Farm or Buckingham Palace. Everything is on a strict schedule, so it's a challenge, having this big event on the last day – but we manage!

During my stay at Holyroodhouse, I do manage to get a bit of a break between engagements, just long enough to pop into Jenners, the local branch of House of Fraser, where I can pick up any bits and pieces that we need. I visit other local shops, too, when time allows, as I like to keep my eyes open for something special or useful for The Queen.

The Palace of Holyroodhouse is open to the public throughout the year and it is well worth a visit. The rooms are still much the same as they were when Mary Queen of Scots was in residence during the sixteenth century. The place is steeped in history – imagine if the portraits in the Picture Gallery could talk!

The reversible pendant of St Andrew is steeped in history.

Above: *The Thistle Robe hat and its impressive plumage!*

Left: *The luscious green Thistle Robe with the cross of St Andrew in pride of place.*

Opposite: *The Queen arrives at St Giles Cathedral, Edinburgh. Notice how beautifully the Page's uniform complements this robe.*

THE STATE OPENING OF PARLIAMENT

The State Opening of Parliament is one of the most important annual engagements of The Queen's year. Of course, Her Majesty has many important roles and engagements, and she takes each one very seriously. The State Opening of Parliament, which dates back to the sixteenth century and in its current form to 1852, usually takes place in November or immediately following a General Election. This annual event officially marks the beginning of a session in Parliament, when Her Majesty will address it in The Queen's Speech, which outlines the laws the government hopes will be approved over the upcoming year. The Queen speaks in the House of Lords on behalf of Her Majesty's Government, with the speech written by the Prime Minister.

A fun fact! During the State Opening of Parliament a hostage from the Houses of Parliament is taken just before The Queen leaves for Parliament and is held at Buckingham Palace. This tradition, which dates back to the reign of Charles I, is a reminder that the Sovereign and Parliament did not always share an easy relationship: the 'hostage' guarantees The Queen's safe return to Buckingham Palace. Rest easy, though: the 'hostage', who is usually the Vice-Chamberlain of The Queen's Household and a government whip, is entertained with tea and biscuits while he or she watches The Queen deliver her speech on television.

Preparing Her Majesty for such a crucial day is by no means easy! There is a lot to do, as well as keeping on top of the normal day-to-day routine during the week that leads up to it, and I try to keep my diary free. A few days before the State Opening my hand-picked specialist team of Assistant Dressers and I prepare the State Robe. First, I ask The Queen's Footman, Ian Robinson, to bring me the long, heavy, airtight black metal box in which it is stored. The box is kept in a room along the corridor on the Dressers' Floor, which also holds the other State Robes, such as the Garter and Thistle Robes, in their boxes. The Queen's military uniforms are kept there, too. Once Ian has brought in the metal

Opposite: The Queen wearing the Imperial State Crown at the State Opening of Parliament.

At Buckingham Palace, before heading to the Houses of Parliament. The State Robe is neatly folded in its velvet bag.

box, he then places it, with assistance, on a table secure enough to take its weight.

We open the box and remove the first few layers of tissue. Then we take out the large square red velvet bag, which is very heavy due to its gold tassels, and rest it over a bolster. The bag was made to carry the robe, once it has been maintained and folded, to the Houses of Parliament.

There is more tissue to remove before we get to the robe. When it was last used, it was placed on a roller, so we lift the robe, including the roller, onto the table, and the box is taken down and put away safely, so no one falls over it; it is solid metal and the corners are sharp.

We then unroll the robe over the table. Once it is fully opened, I look for any holes or bruises to the velvet and any damage to the gold-thread-embellished border. I inspect the collar and cape, which are made from ermine fur, to ensure they are in pristine condition. Then it takes four of us to carry the robe to the ironing board in the workroom, due to its length and weight – one person could not carry it properly. The satin ribbons, which are already stitched to the robe on the shoulders, are checked to make sure they are secure with no loose stitches – they help hold the robe in place on The Queen. The next step is to iron the ribbons – one person ironing and two holding the robe, letting the the rest of it lie on a chair for support. When all the inspections and ironing are completed (around thirty minutes), we leave the robe hanging in a warm room so that any creases in the velvet can fall out. Shortly before the event, we fold the robe and put it inside the red velvet bag.

Her Majesty's elegant fur cape.

On the day before the State Opening of Parliament, I select two State Dresses for Her Majesty to choose from. Before we bring them downstairs to The Queen, my team and I check our diaries from the past couple of years to make sure Her Majesty hasn't worn either of the two options I plan to offer. I try to keep the dress as light as possible as the robe is heavy. The heaviest elements of the robe are the velvet and the gold thread, not the fur. As always, I check the zip, buttons, hooks and eyes, necklines, hems, and sleeves on both dresses.

While one of my team is selecting the handbag and shoes for each dress, I make sure that either a cashmere cape or a fur wrap is available for The Queen to wear over the dress until she must put on the State Robe. I will then choose the jewellery to complement the dress, making sure it fits well in the neckline. There are two special necklaces to choose from – the Collet Necklace, which has matching earrings, or the Jubilee Necklace. The Collet Necklace was created in 1858 for Queen Victoria and is also known as the Coronation Necklace. It is made up of twenty-five cushion-cut brilliant diamonds, which graduate in size, with a large diamond pendant weighing approximately 22.48 carats. Made in 1887 by Carrington & Co, it was presented to Queen Victoria by the 'Women's Jubilee Offering', a group of aristocratic women, to honour her Golden Jubilee. It features a large central pearl and diamond quatrefoil with a pearl and diamond crown at the top and a large pearl drop hanging at the bottom. The remaining necklace has graduated diamond and trefoil lines, six of which could work also as brooches. The jewellery is checked in the diaries: I alternate the necklaces and earrings every year.

Her Majesty The Queen will always wear the Diadem, which is more a diamond headpiece than a tiara, but not a crown. It was originally known as the George IV State Diadem and was made for the monarch in 1820 by Rundell & Bridge. It consists of 1,333 diamonds, which weigh 320 carats, and contains a four-carat yellow

Fastening the robe, using hooks and eyes and press studs.

diamond within the shape of a cross at the front centre: the cross pattée. Along the base there are two strings of pearls, the top strand containing eighty-one and the lower one eighty-eight. It also features diamond-set roses, thistles and shamrocks.

Every queen and queen consort from the reign of William IV onwards has worn the Diadem. During Queen Victoria's reign, the Diadem was reset with jewels from the Royal Collection. Queen Elizabeth II wore it to go to her Coronation and always wears it during the procession to and from the State Opening of Parliament in her gold coach.

My team and I have an early start on the morning of the State Opening of Parliament, and the weather can usually be better – it never seems to be sunny on that day! First, the girls and I take the State Robe from where it is hanging and place it on the long table, where we fold it up very carefully. This job takes four people, and it has to be done in a particular order to ensure it fits into the velvet bag correctly.

First, we fold the sides into the middle, then fold them once more into the centre, which makes the robe much narrower. Next, we take the bottom and fold it about 2 feet in. We keep making 2-foot folds until we almost reach the top.

Finishing touches.

*Note the placement
of the chairs to support
the extraordinary
weight of the robe
as it is fastened on.*

*A little gin and water
come in handy to give the
diamonds extra sparkle*

The top of the robe, the ermine cape and collar, is folded back so it is resting on the velvet folds. This enables me to position the ribbons carefully so they are not creased in transit. Now I can slip the robe into the red velvet bag. The gold tassels are pulled slightly to close it. Once this is complete, I place the bag outside The Queen's private rooms, where it is safe and ready for me to take to the Houses of Parliament later that morning.

We are all raring to go.

Once I have woken Her Majesty and checked everything in the dressing room is in order for her to dress, I go back upstairs and have a quick cup of my favourite Yorkshire tea – my only cup of tea until we return to Buckingham Palace after the speech has been delivered. Shortly after this, The Queen will ring and I, along with the other Dressers, will go down to The Queen's dressing room where I will discuss with Her Majesty anything she requires for the day, after which The Queen will go for breakfast.

The final preparations can then begin. I bring the two dresses that have been chosen to The Queen's dressing room, while the Assistant Dressers prepare the shoes, handbag, cape, and gloves. I always choose the jewellery the day before, to save myself time in the morning, and also in case there are any changes to the programme. The jewellery always includes the Diadem, earrings, necklace, watch, bracelet, and rings. I lay everything on the jewellery tray that once belonged to Queen Mary. At this point I will take the jewellery away and give it a final clean and polish. A little gin and water come in handy to give the diamonds extra sparkle – just don't tell the jeweller! – and a drop of washing-up liquid and water will get rid of any hairspray stains. The Queen's Jeweller will give the stones a deep clean when necessary, so for me it's just a matter of a quick polish and they're sparkling once more. I return the tray and place it on a small table next to The Queen's dressing table. I will take a last look at everything and, satisfied that all is correct and ready for The Queen, I thank my team of Dressers, knowing I can confidently leave them to help Her Majesty get ready for this grand occasion.

The Queen's Page – either Paul Whybrew or Barry Mitford – and I then depart for the Houses of Parliament. The Queen's Page will carry the red velvet bag containing the robe, while I carry the famous Collar and the Great George of the Order of the Garter, which is worn for the State Opening of Parliament as well as the Garter Day service. We are taken by car along Birdcage Walk to Westminster; it is an exciting but nervous journey, as all I can think about is whether The Queen has everything she needs. Once The Queen gets into her coach, there is no going back. The ceremony is transmitted on live television, so there is no room for mistakes.

The Queen's Page and I arrive at the Houses of Parliament and make the climb up the long staircase to the Robing Room. Red screens stand open across the far corner of the room with just enough space for a dressing table, a small table and two normal-sized chairs. There is also just enough room for four Pageboys to lift the robe once Her Majesty is finally ready.

When I am in the Robing Room waiting for The Queen's arrival, I am surrounded by beautiful tapestries, silks, and paintings illustrating the legends of King Arthur. It is majestic, breathtaking, and the excitement builds as we all wait for the arrival of Her Majesty.

There is a small television in the Robing Room, where we all watch The Queen leave Buckingham Palace. There is no sound, but we can see The Queen sitting in her gold coach, making her way towards the Houses of Parliament. I am still going over everything in my head at this point: was it all ready for The Queen as I'd planned – gloves, the right shoes, the correct handbag, the white fur wrap and the white cashmere cape as an alternative?

I go behind the privacy screens and place two chairs in the middle of that space. Although the area is small, we always manage. There is just enough room to manoeuvre, to lay the Collar on the table and secure to it the Lesser George badge. I unfold the State Robe and place it over the two chairs. This is no easy task: the two chairs will take the main weight of the robe, which makes it easier for me to lift the front, the Collar and cap, which overlaps the velvet at the top of the robe, then place it on The Queen's shoulders.

Once Her Majesty has arrived, she joins me behind the screens, which I then close. The Queen removes the Diadem and her gloves and places them on the dressing table and I start to arrange the robe on her. We are silent, concentrating hard. The process of fitting it is complex and I have little time to achieve it – usually around five minutes. It is very difficult to get under the robe because of the way it is placed on The Queen's shoulders. I must lift the front and raise it on to my right shoulder, taking some of the weight, then place it above The Queen's shoulders. Her Majesty is then able to position the robe herself and manoeuvre it so it is comfortable. There are two fairly wide satin straps with hooks and eyes on each side of the robe, which are pulled under The Queen's arms, and hooked together tightly so the robe stays in place.

Once this is done, and with Her Majesty's help, I put the Collar over her head. The Queen always helps by holding it on the other side, making it much easier for me to lift it over her head. Once the Collar is placed on The Queen's shoulders on the ribbed under ribbons, and I am happy that it is in the correct position, with the Lesser George in the middle of The Queen's waist, I count four of the medallions from the middle to the shoulder, and tie the under ribbons in smaller bows to secure the Collar, ensuring it cannot move. I move on to the wider satin ribbons, taking one near Her Majesty's neckline and bringing it over the Collar and across to her shoulder. I feed this ribbon in and out through the Collar to secure it even more firmly, then tie a larger bow. The robe is now fitted and ready.

On one occasion, quite soon after I'd started working for Her Majesty, I just froze. I held up her robe as normal, hooked it up and lifted the Collar over her head. I counted four medallions up the Garter Chain and attached it. I was in the middle of feeding the ribbons in and out of the links of the Collar when I froze. I simply couldn't move. I don't know why it happened – I think I must have been overwhelmed by the significance of the occasion, or perhaps nerves got the better of me – but I could hear whispering outside the screened area, people wondering what was happening. I started to worry that I was holding up The Queen and the ceremony. Then Her Majesty touched my hand where it lay on her shoulder, and said to me quietly and gently, 'Don't worry, just take your time. Take your time.' I apologised profusely, of course, then took a deep breath, picked up that ribbon and carried on. Her Majesty had calmed my nerves and she was soon ready to go.

Once the robe is secured, I pull the red screens slightly apart, just wide enough for the Lord Great Chamberlain to present The Queen with her Imperial State Crown on a red cushion. The Queen takes the crown from him and moves slightly towards the mirror on the table, then I close the screens once more. Her Majesty places the crown on her head and secures it by twisting it from side to side. It is heavy, weighing just over 2 pounds (1 kilogram) and sits perfectly with no need of support or clips. This all takes place while the heavy back part of the robe continues to rest over the two chairs. Once The Queen is satisfied the crown is sitting comfortably on her head, she puts her gloves back on. I open the screen once more to allow the Pageboys, who have been waiting patiently in the room, to come in and take up the satin handles on the sides of the robe. The boys are lovely, although understandably nervous and sometimes quite shy, but they have been trained in what to do and always carry out their duties carefully and well. They are chosen from the Royal Family, the Royal Household and friends. As they lift the robe I move the chairs to one side, so that they can position themselves behind The Queen with no obstacles in their way.

The Queen will chat with the boys for a few moments to make them feel at ease, and while this is happening, His Royal Highness The Duke of Edinburgh will take his place at the right-hand side of The Queen. Prince Philip has undertaken this role every year except for in 2017, when The Prince of Wales escorted Her Majesty. Taking his arm, they walk together towards the large wooden doors. The first two Pages will start to move at the same time as The Queen so that the robe moves smoothly. The back two Pages step forward,

The Queen and the Duke of Edinburgh walk through the Royal Gallery in the Palace of Westminster before the State Opening of Parliament in 2010.

keeping the robe off the floor, and follow carefully. They have to let the robe sink a little so it does not pull The Queen backwards, and they must keep to the same pace as The Queen and The Duke of Edinburgh. The Prince of Wales and The Duchess of Cornwall follow them, then The Queen's Ladies-in-Waiting.

The large wooden doors to the House of Lords' chamber open at exactly 11am and The Queen, The Duke of Edinburgh and the Royal entourage make their way to the throne. This is where Her Majesty will deliver her speech on behalf of her government.

As soon as they leave, I feel relieved, but only briefly: the very moment the doors shut behind Her Majesty I start to worry – will the crown stay on? Is the dress too long? Throughout the ceremony, I hold my breath and watch on the silent monitor, waiting for Her Majesty to come back through the doors safely so I can breathe again.

Once the speech is over, I have the screens open, waiting for The Queen, His Royal Highness and the Pages to return. Only The Queen and the Pages will enter the area behind the screens, and everyone else waits on the other side. I place the two chairs back in position before The Queen returns so that the Pages can return the robe to them, then the boys take their leave of Her Majesty and she thanks them. I close the screen behind the boys and Her Majesty takes off the Imperial State Crown, which she places back on its cushion.

Next I begin to untie the larger ribbons and release the smaller ones from the Collar. Again, Her Majesty will help me lift the Collar over her head, bringing it forward so I can take the weight of the St George and Dragon badge and the chain, and then I place it on the table. Next, I manoeuvre the robe onto my shoulder and unfasten it from behind The Queen's arms, so that it can slowly slide off her shoulders and rest safely on the chair. And what a relief that must be! One would never know it, but it has been digging in under The Queen's arms for about twenty minutes from start to finish.

I open the screen for The Queen to pass the crown and cushion back to the Lord Great Chamberlain. The Queen thanks him, he bows his head to her, and takes his leave, to return the crown to the Tower of London. The screens are closed once more. The Queen is now able to put on the Diadem again, her stole or cape and gloves. I open the screens one final time and The Duke of Edinburgh is ready to take The Queen back to Buckingham Palace in the Gold State Coach.

Once everyone has left I unscrew the St George and Dragon pendant from the chain and place it in its red velvet box. Then The Queen's Page and I take away the chairs and lay the robe flat on the floor. For now, I can fold it quickly so it fits well into the red velvet bag, ready to be correctly folded and carefully returned to storage later when we are back at the Palace and have more time. I gather together the bits and pieces from the dressing table into a small bag, and we are ready to go. The Queen's Page and I return by car to Buckingham Palace, looking at each other with relief. Phew! We are so glad when it's over.

Her Majesty places the crown on her head and secures it by twisting it from side to side.

THINGS AREN'T ALWAYS WHAT THEY APPEAR TO BE

The State Opening of Parliament in 2017 was delayed due to the General Election and was rescheduled for 19 June. That was the same date as Garter Day, which had to be cancelled that year.

It was also decided that Her Majesty would not wear her traditional State Opening of Parliament Robe or long dress, but would wear a day dress instead. The Queen has worn her Imperial State Crown every year, except in 1974 and on this particular occasion. The change was made because the engagements diary was so busy for everyone involved that a simpler form of the ceremony that would work for all those involved was put forward and agreed.

I already had in stock some material suitable for Her Majesty's outfit, so after I'd checked the background against which The Queen would be sitting – to be sure that the colours wouldn't clash – I made the design and passed it, with my instructions, to the in-house dressmaker. Then the milliner, Stella, and I sat down with a cup of tea to discuss the design of the hat.

We chose a Breton-brim block style, which would create an upturned brim, so Her Majesty's face could be clearly seen, and The Queen could see everyone in the room. We chose a large square crown to balance the brim and five flowers, made from feathers with tiny seed pearls, painted yellow. It never occurred to Stella and me that people might think we were copying the European Union flag. The press and the rest of the media were quick to assume that was the case. I understand from reading the papers and seeing all the articles online that there was almost a meltdown on social media with people speculating that The Queen's outfit and hat paid tribute to the EU flag, and that The Queen was making a subtle statement about the recent Brexit vote. It was a coincidence but, boy, did it attract a lot of attention, and it certainly made us smile.

It was a coincidence

Opposite: *Her Majesty delivers the Queen's Speech during the State Opening of Parliament in 2017. The hat has since been altered – see page 111.*

THE ROYAL VARIETY PERFORMANCE

Among all the formal engagements that Her Majesty attends each year, there is one that has perhaps just a little more glitz and glamour than the others: the Royal Variety Performance. Founded in 1912, this televised variety show raises money for the Royal Variety Charity, of which The Queen is a patron, and features performances from comedians, singers, dancers, and sometimes even magicians. I know it is one of the highlights of Her Majesty's year, and in 2009, I had the honour of attending too.

That particular year, the event was held in the Grand Opera House in Blackpool and, as always, I wanted to create something special for Her Majesty to wear. In fact, I had decided that it might be fitting to design something a little bit different for The Queen, considering that the Royal Variety Performance is an evening unlike any other. I knew that I had some beautiful black material in the stockroom that would make the perfect evening dress – it sparkled and shimmered just the right amount and I knew that it would catch the light perfectly in the flashes from the photographers' cameras. With a wave-like striped pattern running vertically down the fabric, I knew the design of the dress needed to be simple so that the subtle yet beautiful material could be showcased. I was thrilled that The Queen liked my provisional designs as it had struck me that Her Majesty rarely wore black to glamorous occasions like this and it suits her so wonderfully.

On the night of the performance, I was so excited to be attending and I travelled to the Opera House with the Equerry and the Lady-in-Waiting. I began to get more and more nervous as we approached as this was one of the first engagements I had been invited to attend with Her Majesty and The Duke of Edinburgh. The Equerry reassured me and told me to relax and enjoy myself, but as our car pulled up, I was totally taken aback by how many people were outside on the street and nearly fell flat on my face trying to get out of the car elegantly in my long evening dress.

Opposite: The Queen during the Royal Variety Performance in 2009.

Safely inside the venue and in my seat, I was struck by how electrifying the atmosphere was. My seat was near the Royal Box and I had to keep pinching myself that this was real. As the evening went on, we were lucky enough to see performances from Katherine Jenkins, the dance troupe Diversity, and Michael Bublé. However, I really could not contain myself when Ms Bette Midler came onto the stage. My heart stopped when she walked out. I was so overwhelmed with emotions. I had to remind myself where I was because I wanted to stand up and cheer. Composure, Angela!

Ready and excited for the evening!

I knew Her Majesty loves music and that she would be much more composed than I was when Ms Midler sang 'The Wind Beneath My Wings', which always makes me so emotional as it reminds me of my family, who are truly the wind beneath my wings. It really was a special evening, so different to any of Her Majesty's other annual engagements and it was a thrill to be able to witness everything from right next to the Royal Box. Before Bette Midler sang she said, 'Tonight is a dream come true for me.' This was also my dream coming true, and what a night to remember.

The Queen meets
singer Bette Midler
and musician Jake
Shimabukuro
following the Royal
Variety Performance.
Performance in 2009.

CHRISTMAS AT SANDRINGHAM HOUSE

Every year The Queen spends Christmas and New Year at Sandringham House, in Norfolk. It was bought by Queen Victoria and Prince Albert in 1862 for their son, The Prince of Wales, Albert Edward, as they wanted him to have a quiet place in the countryside where he could go when he needed a rest from his busy London schedule.

The Prince of Wales, who became King Edward VII, rebuilt Sandringham House as he needed a larger home for his growing family and more bedrooms for when he had guests. Throughout his life, The King continued to improve not only the house, but also the Estate. When he died, Sandringham House stayed in the Royal Family and is now home to Her Majesty The Queen, who thoroughly enjoys being there with her family throughout the Christmas period until after 6 February, the anniversary of her father's death. Like Balmoral, Sandringham is for holidays, although spending time at either house isn't all that relaxing as there is a lot to do, and many events to attend. The Queen is just as busy as she would be in London, with more guests to entertain. There may be several outfit changes in one day – it could be as many as five or even up to seven, although that is rare – depending on the number of planned engagements, as well as the weather and temperature, which can change so quickly around Sandringham. It can be beautiful one day and freezing the next. Thankfully, the House Foreman and his team ensure the house is well maintained, so inside it is always warm.

I always use the same bedroom during my time there, so it's easy for me to settle in when I arrive. My room also becomes my office, so I have a desk and computer tucked away in the corner. I have a lovely view of the gardens from my window so I can see what the weather is doing; then, with the prevailing conditions in mind, I can choose appropriate outfits each day for The Queen.

In the mornings, before breakfast, The Queen will either put on a skirt and blouse or will choose to wear a day dress from her wardrobe in her dressing room. Once Her Majesty has had breakfast, she will meet with her Private

The Queen attends St Mary Magdalene Church in Sandringham every Christmas Day.

Secretary or have a private audience. After the meetings, Her Majesty may change for lunch if there are guests staying in the house. Sometimes when a Royal Shoot is taking place, The Queen will attend the shooting lunch. This means she needs to change into her shooting gear, which is a lengthy process for anyone! This outfit is all about warmth and comfort – and the layers. First the trousers go on, then waterproof trousers over the top, then a long-sleeve shirt, jumper, and cardigan, thick socks so feet stay warm and dry and, finally, Wellington boots. Last, Her Majesty picks up her gloves, scarf, and waterproof mac to head out in the car to meet the shooting party.

After lunch, which takes place at one of the lodges on the Estate, The Queen will return to Sandringham House and will either change into a skirt and blouse if she is taking the dogs out or, if guests are staying in, into a dress for afternoon tea. Between all of the wardrobe changes The Queen makes time throughout her day to deal with all the paperwork and answer letters that come to her in the red boxes. She is always busy at work and never seems to tire.

In the afternoon I lay out sketches of evening dresses for The Queen to look through and choose what she would like to wear that evening and, occasionally, she may have to pick out a dress for a cocktail party. Once Her Majesty has chosen her dress for dinner, a handwritten notice is pinned up in the Dressers' Corridor detailing what she will be wearing, so that The Queen's ladies' maids can select an appropriate dress for the lady they are looking after. When it comes to the Royal Family, it doesn't matter if they wear the same colour as The Queen because they are family, and sometimes the ladies will wear cocktail dresses even though The Queen might be wearing a long one. Other guests, though, feel they shouldn't be in the same colour as Her Majesty, although The Queen would not mind if this did happen. So we try to help The Queen's ladies' maids as often as we can. The Housekeeper makes sure the service given to all of The Queen's guests and staff is of the highest standard.

If The Queen was hosting a cocktail reception for the Estate staff, Her Majesty would change into a cocktail dress. Nothing too sparkly, just a smart silk dress: The Queen would not want her guests to feel underdressed: they are likely to be wearing suits and tea dresses. However, if it is a larger cocktail party, it would be a more formal, sparkly dress. The guests like to dress up, too. The guests, who are usually friends and family, are given a bit of guidance as to what they need to pack before they arrive, although most of those who come to stay have been before and know what to expect.

If the reception goes on until 7.30pm and The Queen feels comfortable, she will remain in the cocktail dress and not worry about changing into evening dress. Alternatively, if she wants to change for dinner, Her Majesty will wear

The Queen riding at Sandringham.

a long evening gown. Dressing for dinner is
a tradition The Queen Mother kept up after
the death of King George V, when she would
wear a long evening dress, and The Queen has
followed her example. This is when Her Majesty's
beautiful jewellery comes out.

Once I know which dress The Queen will
be wearing, I ask her if she would like to wear
diamonds or pearls. In my first book, *Dressing The
Queen*, I went into more detail about her jewellery,
and how I make the decisions when offering her
jewellery selection. So, if The Queen chooses
a red dress, I wouldn't offer rubies because
they would disappear on the dress, suggesting
diamonds instead. If a dark or black dress was
chosen, rubies are a beautiful match. If the
dress is pale blue I would offer aquamarines or
diamonds, or sometimes, just to soften the colour
of the dress, I would offer a lovely set of pearls.
It all depends on the colour and style of the dress
and, of course, the cut of its neckline. Imagine
having such spectacular jewellery to wear and
knowing the history behind each piece.

The dress and jewellery are laid out for Her
Majesty, along with a choice of shoes. If The
Queen is wearing a black dress then black shoes
are offered, or possibly silver. If the dress is red, I

*With the dogs after a
walk at Sandringham
in 1998.*

offer black or silver, but never gold as it would look too Christmassy, although if
the dress had some cream or gold in the material, I might offer gold shoes.

So, Sandringham is much loved, especially during the Christmas season. The
house is buzzing and I love to hear the children running around, laughing and
playing. It looks magical, too, with the tree and all of the Christmas decorations.

The Queen attends church with her family every year on Christmas Day.
Christmas is such a special time of year – everyone puts on their best clothes
and, of course, The Queen is no different. There is so much media coverage,
with pictures sent all over the world, and I take a lot of care in designing Her
Majesty's outfit. I start to plan well in advance – around two months or so
– checking to see what colours The Queen wore in previous years as I don't
want to repeat a colour for a few years. I always think of the children and the

other members of the public who are standing outside, waiting patiently for Her Majesty's arrival at the church. I like to make sure The Queen is wearing a festive colour so the well-wishers can see her easily. I do alternate years with Stewart Parvin, so we each get a turn making The Queen look lovely on Christmas Day.

The Queen attends the Christmas Day church service in 2017.

*A warm, vibrant outfit
for a chilly Christmas
morning.*

THE CHRISTMAS MESSAGE

So many people want to see what The Queen wore to church on Christmas Day but, of course, there are many more across the country and around the world who look forward to The Queen's Christmas Message. It's an important part of Christmas Day for many people – something to be enjoyed after a long lunch and a time to reflect on the events of the year. It's a privilege for me to be involved in this significant occasion.

As part of the preparations for the speech, I am in touch with the broadcasters a couple of weeks before filming. I've got to know them quite well over the years – at the BBC, ITV, and Sky – and we've developed a smooth process for making sure everything goes perfectly. Firstly, I ask what colours and decorations they're planning to use for the scene and they'll give me a detailed description, including which furniture will be featured and how the tree will be decorated. I then pick out a selection of outfits for The Queen that might be suitable, based on the colours chosen for the setting. Ultimately, I leave it up to the production team to decide on the final outfit as the camera crews and producers know what will work and what won't: red, for example, is difficult to capture on camera, and in green, Her Majesty might disappear into the background, depending on the positioning of the tree.

In 2012, to celebrate Her Majesty's Jubilee year, as well as the eightieth year since King George first broadcast his speech over the radio, the production company suggested that it might try something a bit different. The Queen is always willing to embrace technology, so it was agreed that for the first time the Christmas message would be broadcast in 3D. On the day of filming, nothing was noticeably different with the cameras, and Her Majesty was as professional as ever, with the speech captured in one take.

It's a very rare occasion when someone else decides what The Queen will wear, particularly on such a significant day! But I trust the television crews and we work brilliantly as a team. Of course, I'll discuss their choice with Her Majesty, but if I'm assured that it's the right decision, she is satisfied. The only other thing left for me to do is to arrange for the make-up artist, Marilyn Widdess, to be there on the day of filming. You might be surprised to know that this is the only occasion throughout the year when Her Majesty does not do her own make-up.

This is the only occasion throughout the year when Her Majesty does not do her own make-up.

Opposite: *The Queen recording her Christmas Day message in 2018. The Duke of Edinburgh designed this brooch in 1966 for Her Majesty in the shape of a scarab, wrought in gold, rubies, and diamonds.*

CHAPTER 3

The Eyes of the Nation

THE CHRISTENING ROBE

I would like to dedicate this story to Barbara Buckfield, better known as June

Every day I am concerned, first and foremost, with the design and maintenance of Her Majesty's wardrobe. The Queen's outfits are always my top priority, but now and again the opportunity arises for me to assist with the Royal wardrobe in a more unusual way. Needless to say, it's always a pleasure to help with an exhibition of iconic Royal gowns, but a few years ago I had the honour of undertaking a once-in-a-lifetime task.

After 163 years of use, the famous Royal Christening Robe had been worn by sixty-two members of the Royal Family since its first outing in 1841 at the christening of Queen Victoria's eldest daughter, Princess Victoria. Made of Spitalfields silk and intricate Honiton lace, it was an extremely delicate piece that had historically never been washed after each wearing, other than a light spot clean with fresh spring water. After the christening of Lady Louise Windsor, the daughter of the Earl and Countess of Wessex, in 2004, I had noticed that, after so many years of use, the robe had snagged on bracelets and watches, and had acquired quite a few stains along the way. As I was preparing to put it away, I mentioned to Her Majesty that if it was worn again it might become irreparable. This evidently stayed with The Queen because the next time we were alone together she asked if I would make a replica of the robe for future use so that the original could be locked away safely.

Touched that Her Majesty had entrusted such an important task to me, I set about making a plan. My first task was to examine the existing robe in detail, so I removed most of the furniture in my workroom except for a good-sized table and laid the robe carefully on top. My first thought was that it was the most beautiful garment I had ever seen. The detail that had gone into the different

The Queen asked if I would make a replica of the robe

Opposite: Queen Victoria at the christening of her great-grandson, the future King Edward VIII, with the baby's mother, Mary of Teck, and grandmother Alexandra.

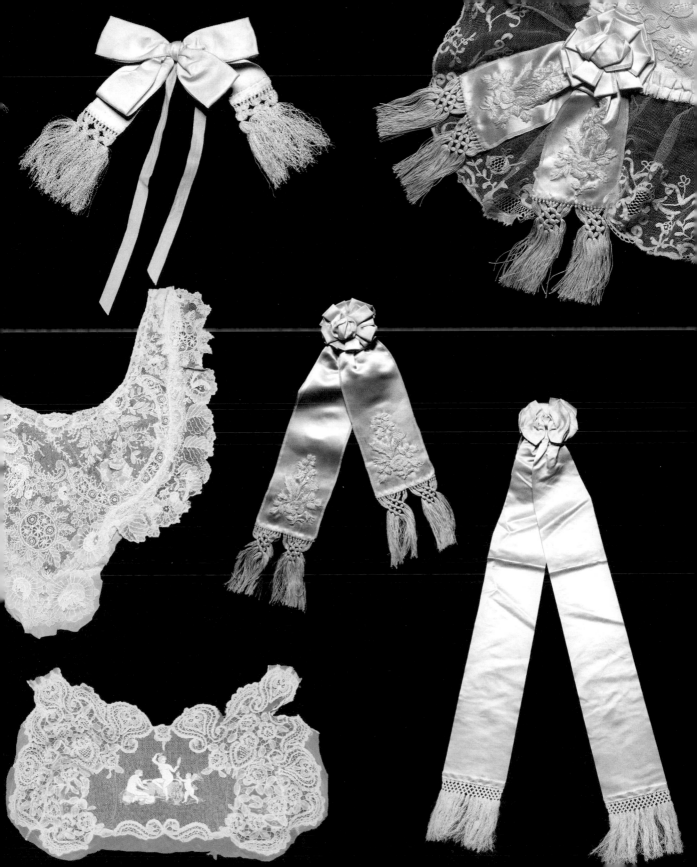

sections of lace was extraordinary, particularly considering that a square inch of Honiton lace can take ten hours to make. The sheer quantity of lace, too, was amazing, delicately folded to give the effect of a full skirt beneath the magnificent bodice and sleeves. At the time, due to the available lighting and other working conditions, it would have taken at least a year, perhaps even eighteen months, to create. I had heard that it was styled after Queen Victoria's wedding dress and I could see the resemblance. It was heartbreaking to see such a beautiful creation deteriorate, and I was determined to produce something equally lovely that could be worn by many future generations to come.

Thankfully, there was no news of any Royal babies in the near future, as I knew it would take several months to source the finest materials, draw the designs, and create the robe. The project was to be kept top secret, so it was a happy coincidence that a new dressmaker joined our team and turned out to be the perfect ally. June Buckfield, whose real name was Barbara, had applied for the position after working for Jaeger. She was due to retire after many years with them, and after I'd interviewed many candidates, it was obvious that she was the right person for the job, bringing valuable experience to the team, as well as her workmanship, and I knew that her personality would fit right in with the rest of us. Shortly after her arrival, I told her about the secret task of recreating the Christening Robe and she was thrilled to be involved. However, shortly afterwards, June was sadly diagnosed with terminal cancer and needed treatment immediately. I made sure to let her know that as soon as her treatment was over she could come straight back to the Palace to help me with the robe.

First I had to find a lace-maker to replicate the main bodice exactly, as this would undoubtedly be the most time-consuming material to produce. I required three types of lace but the majority was to be used in the full, layered skirt of the robe. There was also to be a slight alteration to the frill, at the request of The Queen. I initially spoke to a well-known company based on the outskirts of London but unfortunately, and much to my surprise, they were not very interested and quoted an enormous amount of money. Knowing that Her Majesty is always mindful of cost, I approached Joel & Son Fabrics; the owner, Mrs Bull, and her colleague Linda told me about a small family business in Italy called Vema that specialised in making the finest lace and embroidery. I made a call to Paola Mazzucchelli and asked for a quote based on the quantity I would need. Paola gave an approximate cost, which was much more reasonable, but said she would need to see the garment to make sure the firm could commit to the project.

Her Majesty was happy for me, Mrs Bull, and Linda to travel to Italy to visit Vema, but before we went I wanted to take my own measurements of the robe. I knew the lace-makers would be taking their own exact measurements but I wanted

Previous page: The Queen Victoria Christening Robe. Not all of these elements (the cape, the bibs, the medallions, and the ribbons) have been used as often in more recent times – mainly the robe and the bonnet.

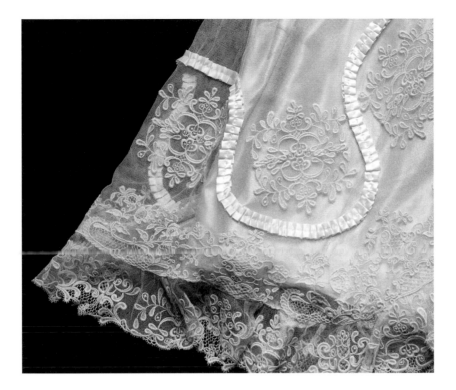

to make sure they were recorded in the Royal Household, too, to help future generations when the time came for another replacement to be made. Measuring a complex garment like that can be difficult; first I had to find its centre point, a length of 70 centimetres from top to bottom, and then I broke the garment down into five sections and rebuilt it to form a gradual gradient across the front. Centimetre by centimetre, I meticulously took note of the dimensions, which was a very useful exercise in understanding how the robe had been put together.

Before long, Mrs Bull, Linda, and I were on our way to Italy. Three ladies on a secret mission. When we arrived, after settling into our hotel, we went to Vema where we met Paola and her family. We got straight down to business and I showed them the Christening Robe, which I had discreetly brought, wrapped in lots of tissue paper, in a large handbag. When the family saw it, I could tell that they appreciated how special and delicate it was. In fact, they were in awe and held it with the utmost care. Seeing how respectfully and gently they handled it, I knew I had made the right decision in approaching them.

We were shown to their enormous workroom, which contained rows and rows of looms, each around 15 metres long. This was ideal as the robe would

*Above: **The Queen Elizabeth II robe** – note the ribbon is completely handstitched.*

*Following page: **The two robes have never been pictured together before. The Queen Victoria robe is on the left, and the Queen Elizabeth II robe is on the right.***

To make sure it looked authentic, we dyed it in Yorkshire tea.

require 3 metres of lace, so we would have plenty of excess for repairs. With everything in place and the details agreed, we flew home. I remember thinking how extraordinary it was to be sitting on a plane with a garment made for Queen Victoria's children.

Having reassured The Queen that everything was going smoothly, I set about my next task: sourcing additional designs of lace to cover the bodice, sleeves, and trim of the robe. Happily, by this time June had come back to the Palace to join me in the enormous task of recreating the robe. Together, we sourced lace to complement that being made in Italy, and to make sure it looked authentic, we dyed it in Yorkshire tea (which is the strongest, as we all know!). One by one, we placed each piece of lace in a small bowl, from the Dressers' kitchen, filled with cool water and a tea bag, and left it for about five minutes, checking regularly until the colour was perfect. With the lace ready to sew onto the robe, the only material left to source was the duchesse satin to go beneath the lace skirt. Once again, Mrs Bull came to the rescue and, with the help of Dino, at Joel & Son Fabrics, found the perfect satin and tea-dyed it to match the lace June and I had worked on.

Right: *We had to use tea to dye it to get the new robe as close as possible to the original in colour, so it wasn't a 'brand new' bright white.*

Opposite: *We actually made the new robe a little bigger than the original to allow more room as most babies are born a little bigger now than they were back then!*

Now that we had sourced all of the necessary materials and used plenty of tea bags, we were ready to start the painstaking process of producing the robe. Vema had delivered the most exquisite lace, so we were ready to go. I gave June the task of all the hand-stitching, as her attention to detail was second to none. A heavy lace panel edged with additional frilled lace was to be attached to the front, with a wider lace frill sewn on which reached around to the back of the gown. Around the neck, a fine millimetre-wide drawstring ribbon and three tiny 6-millimetre buttons were to be attached and buttonholes made. At the bottom

I'm holding the bonnet. The Queen Victoria robe is on the left and the Queen Elizabeth II robe is on the right, and the size difference between the two can be clearly seen.

of the bodice, just before it meets the skirt, June had to apply two rows of 3-millimetre satin-edged lace to the finish, which encased the same narrow ribbon as that used around the neck to allow the robe to be pulled in at the waist. Finally, the bottom of the gown was to be finished with a scalloped border, slightly frilled, which measured no more than 7 centimetres in height. At each stage of the creative process, I would show our progress to The Queen: first the bodice, then the sleeves attached to the bodice, then the skirt with the under-layers on, and finally the completed robe. Her Majesty was very interested to see how it was developing. So much complex and intricate work was involved that it was a relief to us all when the robe was finally complete. From start to finish, it had taken us, appropriately, nine months. Since completion, it has been worn by James, Viscount Severn, son of the Earl and Countess of Wessex, Savannah and Isla Phillips, the children of Peter Phillips (The Princess Royal's son), Maud Windsor, daughter of Lord Frederick Windsor, Mia and Lena Tindall, the children of Zara (The Princess Royal's daughter), Prince George, Princess Charlotte, and Prince Louis, the sons and daughter of the Duke and Duchess of Cambridge, and most recently by Archie Harrison Mountbatten-Windsor, the son of the Duke and Duchess of Sussex.

I cannot describe how touched I was that Her Majesty asked me to create a replica of this historic robe, and trusted me to take the original to Italy. It is an important garment to her, with lots of personal memories. I feel honoured to have created something that will be worn by future generations of the Royal Family, but it was daunting, making sure that I got it absolutely right. On a personal level, working alongside June, who was caring, warm, dedicated, and an expert seamstress, made the experience all the more special.

'VEMA is a small embroidery company, founded in 1969 by my father, Venanzio Mazzucchelli, who was one of the first Italian entrepreneurs to purchase Swiss embroidery machines in Italy. As a company that manufactures high-end, bespoke embroideries, we often receive 'special orders'.

One day in 2004, we received a call from our good customer Joel & Son Fabrics in London, asking if we could take part in a special project to replicate an ancient fabric – a very important undertaking that was to remain confidential. Of course, we agreed at once with enthusiasm. When we were informed that we would be visited by the Queen's Dresser to replicate the Royal Christening gown . . . well, the surprise couldn't have been bigger.

When Angela pulled out the dress, no one dared to touch it. The magnificent hand embroideries were over 160 years old and although still well-kept, were worn out by usage. The fine yarns crafted by skilled workers had created a masterpiece that seemed impossible to replicate. In the weeks that followed, we did several trials and in the end, we used a technique called superposé which is basically a double embroidery, that gives a three-dimensional effect.

Months went by, and then years, and the project remained as a folder in my dad's desk, together with a picture of him and Angela, of which he was so proud. And then one day, in 2013, I received a phone call from Buckingham Palace – the employee who picked up the phone thought it was a joke. It was Angela, announcing that the gown was to be presented officially for the Christening of the Royal heir, Prince George.

Dad was so proud that Angela invited me to see the robe in Buckingham Palace. He passed away in 2015. At every Christening of the British Royal Family, there is a small fan club here in our offices, sharing pictures and, of course, memories. It makes us feel that we took part in a small piece of history.'

By Paola Mazzucchelli

Vema Ltd

GOOD EVENING, MR BOND

The London 2012 Olympics Opening Ceremony was full of colour, sound, light, and spectacular performance. It took place in The Queen's Diamond Jubilee year, right in the middle of an extremely busy period. However, this event stood out. Thousands of volunteers worked seamlessly, creating perfectly choreographed patterns across the vast floor of the Olympic Stadium. Amid the kaleidoscope of activity, there was one moment when the stadium's 62,000 occupants held their breath in stunned silence: Her Majesty, dressed in a peach, crystal and lace cocktail dress, apparently took a daring leap from a helicopter, skydiving towards the stadium 500 feet below. What an entrance!

There are few occasions on which Her Majesty will agree to break protocol, but in 2011, when film director Danny Boyle approached the Royal Household, he had a request to make that we simply could not refuse. I first heard about Danny's grand plan when Private Secretary Edward Young called me into his room: he wanted to run an idea past me, as well as a thought for a sensational arrival at the Olympic Stadium. Danny wanted to ask Her Majesty to feature in a short film as part of his Olympics opening ceremony. She was to be greeted by James Bond, played by Daniel Craig, in the Palace and seemingly escorted to a helicopter. Mr Bond was there to rescue her from an unknown threat that jeopardised her safe arrival on time at an undisclosed event. Once safely aboard, the helicopter would fly over the Houses of Parliament, receiving a salute from Churchill's statue in Parliament Square, before passing beneath Tower Bridge and swinging north to the Olympic Stadium in Stratford, London. Here, the helicopter door would slide open and 'Her Majesty' would take a daring leap out, skydiving down in perhaps her most dramatic entrance to an engagement ever.

Having listened to Danny's plan, I asked him and Edward to give me five minutes so that I could ask The Queen. I remember the look of shock on Danny's face that I would be asking Her Majesty straight away, but there's no point in waiting around with these things: if she said no, that would be the end of it. I ran upstairs and luckily The Queen was free so I asked if she would be

Opposite: The Queen's Page, Paul Whybrew, does his duty alongside Daniel Craig and The Queen during filming for the opening ceremony of the London 2012 Olympic Games.

prepared to do a surprise performance for the Olympics opening ceremony. She was very amused by the idea and agreed immediately. I asked then if she would like a speaking part. Without hesitation, Her Majesty replied, 'Of course I must say something. After all, he is coming to rescue me.'

I asked whether she would like to say, 'Good evening, James,' or 'Good evening, Mr Bond,' and she chose the latter, knowing the Bond films. Within minutes, I was back in Edward's office delivering the good news to Danny – I think he almost fell off his chair when I said that The Queen's only stipulation was that she could deliver that iconic line: 'Good evening, Mr Bond.'

More than perhaps any other public appearance by Her Majesty, this would take meticulous planning. One crucial factor was the dress The Queen would wear for the momentous skydive. It had to be a bright, solid colour that would stand out as 'Her Majesty' descended into the stadium and also while she was in the stadium surrounded by the vibrant celebrations. I had to be careful not to choose a colour that was strongly associated with any of the participating nations, too, so after much consideration, I chose peach. However, the colour wasn't the only factor, the dress also had to be designed perfectly to allow movement in the skirt as The Queen seemingly flew through the air. Of course, there would be two: one for Her Majesty and one for the jump stuntman, Gary Connery.

Skydiving material – note the bloomers detail to help the stuntman's modesty in the air.

'Of course I must say something. After all, he is coming to rescue me.'

The Queen's show-stopping dress.

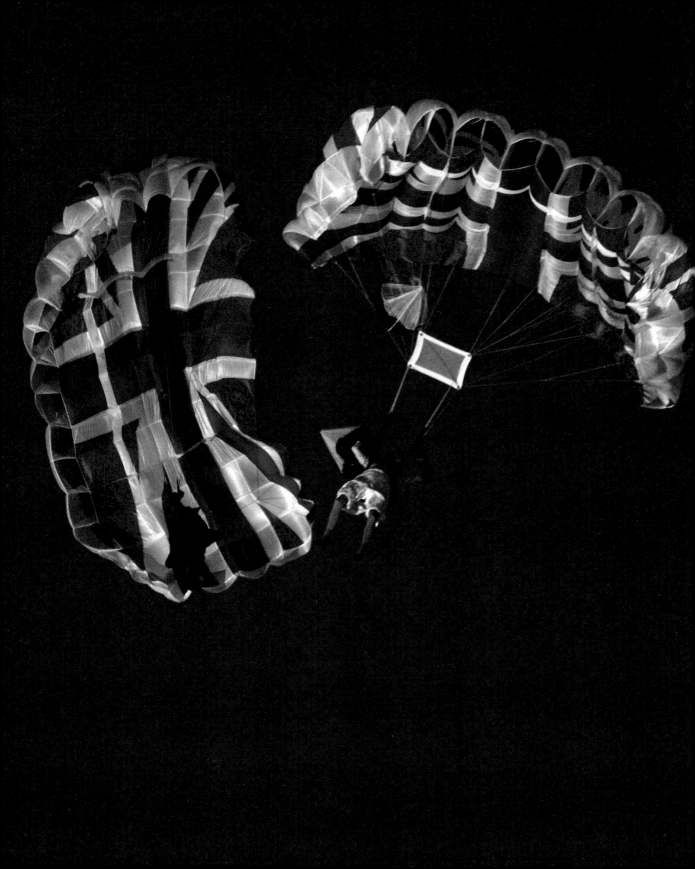

Working closely with Danny's team and the Olympic opening ceremony's costume department, I set about creating two identical versions of the peach dress. For months, the Palace dressmakers worked continuously and discreetly, never allowing both dresses to be visible at the same time. Even other members of the Royal Family were unaware of the plan, so I made up a story that two dresses were needed for an upcoming event, as one was to go on exhibition and I didn't want it to be stained or marked. After much hard work, we eventually finished the stuntman's dress and I delivered it to Danny's team to add the harness and parachute – certainly a first in my years as a dressmaker!

On the day of the filming, I was privileged to watch Her Majesty undertake her role. She was unflappable and even kept 'Mr Bond' waiting for a moment while finishing a letter she was writing. The Queen's Footman, Ian Robinson, outdid himself in his role of animal handler – he managed to align Her Majesty's corgis in the perfect position, using dog biscuits to grab their attention and give the impression that they were watching The Queen's helicopter flying away. The night of the ceremony, of course, was suspense-filled as we all watched to see if Gary, wearing that dress, would land safely just outside the stadium. He did, of course, and Her Majesty resumed her role, walking calmly and coolly to her place after the apparent death-defying leap. I believe she received a standing ovation and it was the perfect contribution to Danny's spectacular vision for the opening of the Games.

Gary Connery parachutes into the stadium.

OUR OWN MONARCH OF THE GLEN

Her Majesty has sat for countless portraits throughout her long reign. Most photoshoots are quite similar, but occasionally an unusual request comes through. I'm always happy to see if Her Majesty might be up for something new.

Back in 2010, Alastair Bruce, a historian and author, had asked Her Majesty if she would consider being photographed by Julian Calder for inclusion in their upcoming book, *Keepers: The Ancient Offices of Britain*. I wasn't at the meeting with Alastair and The Queen, but he came to see me afterwards to explain his suggestion that Her Majesty be pictured on the Scottish moors, near Balmoral. I imagine The Queen had immediately thought about the obvious potential challenge – the Scottish weather. One minute it could be glorious sunshine, but the next there's torrential rain, gusty winds, and thick fog. Alastair asked The Queen if she would think about it for a while, and Her Majesty replied maybe.

As Her Majesty pondered, Alastair approached me to discuss their vision for the outfit she would wear on the moors. Would it be possible for her to wear the Thistle Robe and the Vladimir Tiara as she stood among the Scottish heather? The Vladimir Tiara dates back to 1880, when it was commissioned for the Grand Duchess Vladimir. In 1921, Queen Mary, our Queen's grandmother, had bought it from Princess Nicholas of Greece, the Grand Duchess's only daughter. In 1953 Her Majesty inherited it from Queen Mary. This stunning tiara has fifteen intertwining diamond circles, with either a pearl or emerald suspended from the centre of each. I thought that emeralds would perfectly complement the deep velvet green of the Thistle Robe.

How might Julian and Alastair's plan work if The Queen agreed to go ahead? Her Page, Paul Whybrew, had been told of the request, too, so we put our heads together to find a way to make the iconic photoshoot happen. But, of course, ultimately it was Her Majesty's decision. So, being brave, I asked again whether she might consider it, taking care to explain the plan. If Her Majesty

Previous page: *Julian Calder's photograph,* **Chief of the Chiefs.**

Opposite: *Action!*

got ready in the Castle, we could drive out in her car, stop on the moors, take a few pictures and drive back. The Queen looked at me as though I was crazy. She reminded me that it might easily be pouring with rain or blowing a gale. On top of that, the drive could take up to twenty minutes along bumpy roads – it was not a matter of nipping over to the heather-topped moors. Crossing my fingers, I told her that it wouldn't be raining, and Her Majesty agreed to go ahead. A day was fixed for the photoshoot and now all we had to do was pray that the weather would be kind.

The day before the photoshoot, Paul, Alastair, Julian, and I went out onto the moors to check the location that would work best. Julian and Alastair wanted Her Majesty to stand on a rock, which had a nearly, but not quite, even, flat surface. Returning to the Castle, I went to explain to The Queen that the location for the shoot wasn't too far away and that she would be standing on a slightly uneven rock, but that she would be fine. A couple of photographs, and we'd be on our way back to the Castle.

The day of the photoshoot arrived and we awoke to heavy rain showers. Her Majesty said firmly that she was not going out on the moors in that weather – we would all be soaked through, and the rain would ruin the beautiful velvet Thistle Robe. After a couple of hours, though, blue sky began to break through the grey clouds – the showers were passing. The Queen called for me and said, 'If I do this, we go now.'

It was all hands on deck. I alerted the others and helped The Queen to get ready. In her long gown, tiara, and Thistle Robe, she got into the car and I can only imagine what Her Majesty was thinking as she wrapped and tucked the robe around herself so that she could sit somewhat comfortably. Her face was a picture.

Paul and I followed Her Majesty in the car behind and it only took a short time to drive to the chosen location. Paul, Julian and I helped The Queen out of the car, ensuring that the long robe didn't drag along the rough ground as she walked to the rock on which she was to stand. Some purple heather surrounded it but not quite enough – Paul and I quickly unearthed a few clumps, making sure to keep the soil around the roots, and placed them nearer to Her Majesty. The beautiful green robe was placed in such a way that it gave the impression of flowing down the grassy moors. Holding the Thistle hat, The Queen looked so elegant and regal. It was moving to see our Sovereign standing amid the stunning Highland scenery.

As Julian took his photographs, The Queen kept shooting pointed looks at me and Paul, as if to say, 'Have you seen the sky?' It was getting darker by the minute. Eventually Julian was happy that he had the shot he wanted and, job

The Queen kept shooting pointed looks at me

Previous page: *Notice the heather placement.*

done, we all burst into giggles of relief – even The Queen. Her Majesty removed her tiara and passed it to me with a look that said, 'Are you happy now?', followed by a twinkle in her eye and a beaming smile. We packed up quickly, replanted the heather in its original position, jumped into our cars and the heavens opened as we headed back to the Castle.

Later that day when we were all in The Queen's private rooms, it was clear that she thought the shoot had gone well: and with a grin, she said, 'I really enjoyed that!' Nevertheless, I wouldn't push my luck and ask if she would ever do it again!

Last-minute adjustments – I'm ensuring everything is exact.

BEHIND THE LENS:
ANNIE LEIBOVITZ

Another shoot was particularly memorable, one that captured The Queen in a way that left me awestruck. Back in 2007, the Royal Household commissioned photographs to celebrate The Queen's State Visit to the United States and they wanted this to take place at the same time that Jamestown, Virginia, was celebrating the 400th anniversary of its founding. Annie Leibovitz became the first American photographer to take an official portrait of The Queen . . . four portraits, in fact.

Annie was asked to take four different images of The Queen. In the first, she would be wearing an evening gown with a stole wrapped around her shoulders, sitting down and looking out of an opened window. For the second, she would also be in an evening gown, but wearing a tiara and the Garter Robe, seated again. In the third photograph, she would stand in an evening gown, with a stole draped over her arm. The fourth was to show The Queen wearing her boat cloak that was made famous in Cecil Beaton's powerfully simplistic portrait of Her Majesty, taken in 1968.

For this photoshoot, Annie had a little more freedom than is usual through which to exercise her creativity, and I much enjoyed working with her. I could help by making sure the robe was positioned correctly, when The Queen put it on, so that it showed some of the white silk lining.

When Annie was taking the photograph of The Queen wearing her stole, Her Majesty's pose resembled one of The Queen Mother's, with the fur draped over one shoulder. It didn't look quite right. Instead I suggested that in the picture The Queen might carry it over her arm, as if she was ready to go out but didn't need to put it on yet. Annie agreed, and this became the final shot. Annie was more than happy for me to advise, but that was as far as my role went: I knew Annie was an experienced, professional photographer. She had her own vision, which she captured in the photos she produced. The outcome was amazing.

One of the good things about working in the same job for such a long time is that it allows you to put things right that haven't gone quite as planned in the past. I'm often reminded of this when I think of that photoshoot. Annie had travelled over with her daughter, who would be introduced to The Queen before the portrait sitting. On the day, Her Majesty was scheduled to meet only Annie's daughter and was expecting

Opposite: I was thrilled to be involved in the iconic Annie Leibovitz photoshoot in 2018.

just a handful of people to be present. When The Queen arrived she was met by nearly fifteen people in the room, standing in a straight line, and many members of the press. A misunderstanding meant that footage was captured and broadcast showing The Queen apparently 'storming' out of the photoshoot. This was not an accurate account of what happened. Her Majesty was not 'storming' anywhere: she was making her way to the shoot as planned, and hadn't time to meet so many people. I have always felt so bad for Annie about how this was later reported, as she really didn't deserve to be misrepresented in that way.

Almost nine years later, The Queen and I had a conversation about how we could make things right. Her Majesty's ninetieth birthday was coming up, and I suggested that we invite Annie back to do the official photographs. The Queen was more than happy and in full agreement that it would be the right thing to do to make amends for the earlier misunderstanding, and said yes.

Her Majesty and I discussed different ideas for the photographs. I suggested that Annie should keep things simple and that the shoot should be informal, based around The Queen and her family. I suggested four photographs that should be taken at Windsor Castle: The Queen with His Royal Highness The Duke of Edinburgh; The Queen with all of her great-grandchildren; The Queen with her corgis; and one of The Queen with her daughter, The Princess Royal. I felt that The Queen hadn't been photographed often enough with her daughter and, as I have a daughter myself, I thought it would make a special photo for them to share as mother and daughter. The Queen wholeheartedly agreed.

Soon after, I flew to New York with my assistant, Jackie. I'd never been there before so I was very excited, and we went to see Annie and her team in her studio. When I told her that The Queen had asked for her to return to photograph her on or close to her ninetieth birthday, Annie was thrilled and humbled to receive such an honour.

It was great to see Annie and her team again. After we had spent a little time reminiscing about the 2007 shoot, we got down to work. I explained to Annie how the coming shoot would have to work. Time was limited as the entire Royal Family would be together only during the Easter weekend. We just had a few months to plan everything in detail. I even had the contracts with me for Annie to sign there and then if she agreed. I didn't have any time to waste: everything had to move quickly.

A few weeks later, Annie and her team flew to London to do their own recce with us. We were all so excited and looking forward to seeing the photos. We prayed that the weather would be in our favour on the day. When the day of the shoot arrived, everything went according to plan. Annie captured a stunning image of The Queen and The Duke of Edinburgh, and another of Her Majesty

It would be the right thing to do to make amends

with her daughter, The Princess Royal. The great-grandchildren were all so well behaved, and I think even they were excited about having a group photograph taken with The Queen. But the real stars of the show that day were the corgis! They knew how to work that camera, looking straight at Annie while she was taking the photos. I think they even enjoyed it. I'm sure they were given plenty of special treats afterwards by Ian.

The Queen was delighted with the pictures, which were special family photos to be shared with the public.

Windsor Castle in all its majesty.

THE QUEEN DOING IT HER WAY

I get asked all sorts of questions about my job, with it being unusual – unique, actually. And, of course, everyone is keen to hear about what happens behind closed doors, especially when it comes to Her Majesty, who is beloved in this country and across the world. I'm very careful to respect The Queen's privacy, of course, but one thing I always tell people is just how considerate and thoughtful Her Majesty is – she is always willing to help, never wants to let anyone down, and will always do her best to make sure everyone is content. So, a few years ago, when I had the opportunity to do something special for The Queen, I leaped at the chance.

Many years ago, Her Majesty disclosed something to me – a secret wish that she'd held since she was young. Throughout The Queen's time on the throne, she has been photographed in countless formal ways. However, for a long time, Her Majesty wanted to be photographed more informally and have the freedom, for example, to pose with her hands in her pockets. The Queen Mother and her advisors had always advised against this, suggesting it would not be appropriate, and I believe she has never done this before.

Some years later, when I was writing my first book, *Dressing The Queen*, I remembered Her Majesty's secret wish. Given that the book was all about Her Majesty's outfits and relationship with fashion, I wondered if I might have a wonderful opportunity to make The Queen's wish come true. So, although I was very nervous, I finally asked the question: 'Your Majesty, would you do me a favour? I would like you to consider doing a photoshoot of yourself modelling a dress with your hands in your pockets. It would only be yourself, me, the photographer and his assistant.' The Queen looked at me in amazement as I asked whether she knew the potential implications of the photographs. She didn't take long to answer: yes, she would do it and, yes, she was sure. She asked me to arrange the photographer and I already had someone in mind: Barry Jeffery, whom I trusted implicitly and who I knew would take wonderful pictures.

Her Majesty wanted to be photographed more informally and have the freedom to pose with her hands in her pockets.

Opposite: *A secret wish come true.*

'Just keep
the camera
rolling!'

Shortly after my conversation with The Queen, I went to see Barry and asked if he would like to photograph Her Majesty in a way that she had never been captured before. I explained that I wanted him to photograph The Queen as though she was the most famous model in the world and that she would be posing in a relaxed, informal way. Needless to say, Barry was overjoyed by the idea, and before long, we had booked a date. The photoshoot was to take place in the Throne Room and Her Majesty chose a very fetching white dress, although a crucial element was missing: it had no pockets! Luckily, this was an easy fix, as I had leftover material from when I had made the dress.

The day of the photoshoot arrived. I greeted Barry and his assistant, Gideon, and we walked together, with his camera, to the Throne Room where they set up their equipment. I went to request Her Majesty's company and as soon as she joined us, Barry began to explain his approach and how the photoshoot would progress. Within moments, The Queen raised her hand respectfully and Barry immediately stopped talking. 'No, Barry, this is how we're going to do it,' she said. 'Just keep the camera rolling!' And we were off. Her Majesty took her position in front of the lens and started striking a series of poses, slipping her hands in and out of her pockets and placing them onto her hips, mimicking the stances of a professional model. I stood by in disbelief – The Queen was a natural. Barry and I felt we were experiencing something really special: a moment never to be repeated.

When the photoshoot was over, The Queen and I left the Throne Room and Her Majesty thanked Barry, giving him clear instructions to return the photographs to her. She told me that she was really looking forward to seeing them, and I could tell by her laughter and the twinkle in her eye that she had had a wonderful time.

I was working with the Royal Collection at the time, who were to publish my first book, *Dressing the Queen*, and we were in final discussions regarding the layout, so once the photographs from this special shoot were ready, I handed them over to be placed in the book. However, to my utter amazement and disappointment, I was then told by the Royal Collection that only two photographs would be allowed to be used for the book. Once the full shoot had been shared more widely, their opinion was that these more candid photographs would bring the Monarchy down, and therefore they were not suitable for the public eye. Why they thought that, I have no idea.

The Royal Collection is now under new management, and Mr Tim Knox, who is the director, has been fully supportive of this book and has returned the photographs from this special shoot to The Queen. It is wonderful to have a second opportunity to share the one and only full set of photographs from that exceptional morning, when The Queen's wish was granted and Her Majesty was able to do it her way.

A beautiful portrait, and, I believe, one that is previously unseen.

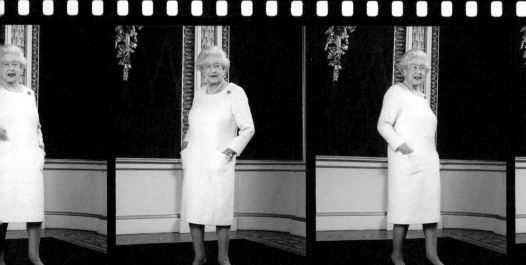

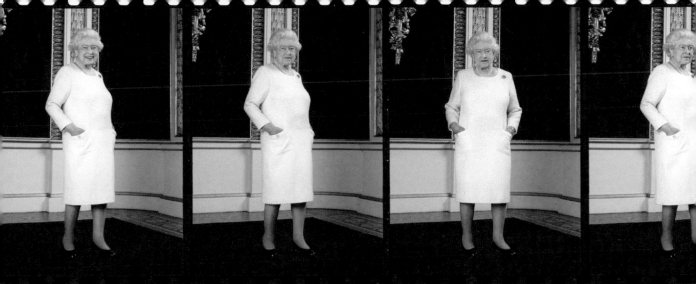

'It was an absolute honour to be asked to photograph The Queen for the cover of the book *Dressing The Queen: The Jubilee Wardrobe*, and the request came as a complete surprise.

At the time I was working on photographing the majority of the content of the book at Buckingham Palace, capturing the magical process that each of Her Majesty's outfits goes through, from fabric selection to the making. I was spending a lot of time with Angela and her team on the Dressers' Floor, following them around on their daily routines, when one day, Angela called me to her office where she asked if I would shoot the book cover picture of The Queen in the Jubilee dress. At that very moment I felt hugely honoured, excited and lucky. What a privilege! It's not something I'd thought I would ever be asked to do.

The day before the shoot, my assistant, Gideon Marshall, and I set up in the Throne Room. It was a surreal experience for us both, especially when we stepped out into the corridor for a break to find Daniel Craig in character as James Bond, standing there, talking on his phone! The scenes for the London 2012 Olympics opening ceremony were being filmed.

On the day of the shoot, naturally I was a little anxious, but I was ready and so was everything else. The moment arrived, and it all went to plan. I managed to capture fantastic shots of Her Majesty in the Jubilee dress and was so pleased with the results. Then The Queen decided she would change her outfit, which was completely unplanned. We had just five minutes to choose a different area to shoot within the Throne Room, move our kit around and be ready for the next shot.

The Queen returned in her second outfit, and we were straight into the flow of shooting, but this session was different, and even more amazing than the first. Everyone was relaxed and having fun. There was lots of laughter, a sense of freedom and movement, which you can see in the series of images.

It was much more like a fashion shoot, and I even captured a shot of The Queen with her hands in her pockets, which was used for the cover of the book. It was a day I'll never forget.

Working with Angela and her team was a once-in-a-lifetime experience. It was fascinating and hugely educational, and Angela was so welcoming. As a photographer, shooting pictures of The Queen was career defining, and something I'd never dreamed of doing. I'd like to thank Angela for making it possible.

And here I am, with Kate, my wife and assistant, being asked once more to produce photographs. This time Angela needs a completely different series of images, to include the original and replica Royal Christening Robes in their full glory and The Queen's Royal Ascot outfits for 2019. I feel so privileged to be asked to return to Buckingham Palace, and so honoured also to share this experience with my wife. I will never forget the magical moments I shared with Angela and her team. '

By Barry Jeffery

Photographer

BEHIND THE LENS: CHRIS LEVINE

Another shoot I remember fondly was for Jersey's 800th anniversary celebration to honour its special relationship with the Monarchy. To reflect this occasion, the Jersey Heritage Trust asked Chris Levine and Robert Munday to work together to create something spectacular.

A unique and extraordinary sitting took place in November 2003 for a holographic portrait: The Queen's picture was going to be turned into a hologram. So much work went into setting up the Yellow Drawing Room in Buckingham Palace as a photographic studio – it took about three days for all the equipment to be installed. Robert designed and built the special camera system, as well as the tracks the camera was going to be sitting on so that it would capture thousands of pictures every minute!

Chris had a particular vision of the shot in mind, and when we discussed his ideas before the sitting, we also talked about outfits. I showed Chris a few options, and he selected the dress he thought would be best for the portrait. The Queen would also be wearing the Diadem, a pearl necklace and a lovely pair of diamond and pearl earrings. Chris asked if I could bring a couple of cloaks and capes with me, as one of the capes he was hoping The Queen would wear was the adapted Officer's Cape of the Life Guards, of which Her Majesty is Colonel-in-Chief.

The day finally came and I had the pleasure not only of helping The Queen dress, but also of seeing the astonishing pieces of equipment that would be used to create the hologram of Her Majesty. How cameras have come on since the Polaroid! I followed The Queen into the Yellow Drawing Room and the room was dark as all of the curtains had been closed. Built in a half-moon across the floor was what looked like a railway track with a camera sitting on it. It reminded me of the old-fashioned coal trucks that were pulled by trains many years ago. It was intriguing!

The Queen listened intently as Chris and Robert explained how this unusual sitting was going to work. Once everyone was happy with the plan, I followed The Queen to the mirror, handed her the Diadem and watched as she carefully placed it on her head. Her Majesty then made herself as comfortable as she could on the chair that was waiting for her. I placed the white-fur-trimmed cape around her shoulders and we were good to go. Lights, camera, action!

During the sitting Chris asked The Queen to sit perfectly still for eight seconds as the series of images was taken. Once the eight seconds had passed, The Queen was able to close her eyes and rest for a moment. The lights were bright, so I know I would have appreciated that if I had been sitting in front of the camera. The Queen looked so peaceful with her eyes closed, and I thought the title of the hologram portrait was fitting. It was called *Equanimity*, as Chris wanted to demonstrate how one could achieve a sense of calm when sitting still and how liberating this could be.

The camera on the tracks took more than 10,000 individual images, which were then converted into the hologram. I was overwhelmed to be given one of the holograms and I have treasured it ever since, carefully packed away for safe keeping.

Actually, the photograph used on the cover of this book was taken during that sitting by Nina Duncan, Chris Levine's assistant. In that picture I am helping The Queen put the Admiral's Boat Cloak – it was made for her in 1968 – over her shoulders, making the final adjustments and ensuring that her pearl necklace was lying straight. I thought that photograph of The Queen and myself was the perfect picture for this book.

Opposite: *The Queen posing for the holographic portrait,* Equanimity, *which was commissioned by Jersey Heritage to commemorate 800 years of allegiance to the crown.*

'A week before my sitting with Her Majesty, I received a phone call from the
Palace. It was Angela Kelly asking me what I would like The Queen to wear
for the Jersey portrait. Until that point, I had been preparing for the shoot
under the impression that I would only find out what Her Majesty would be
wearing on the day itself. I had to pick myself up from the floor – Angela was
suggesting that I could style Her Majesty myself, which was an immensely
exciting but also extremely daunting prospect. Creatively, I was looking to
simplify and purify the work – to create something resonantly modern and
iconic – like The Queen herself – so the choice of attire was critical. Who
better to collaborate with than Angela!

Meeting with Angela at the Palace, I was able to share my thoughts about the work and what I was hoping to achieve artistically. Based on our discussions, she then selected several dresses for us to consider, but in the end I went for a simple, dark blue, A-line number. Angela also suggested that a cape could be fitting, so I asked for a variety of options, knowing that on the day we could change the look very quickly by simply switching capes. In terms of jewellery, along with Her Majesty's diamond and pearl earrings, I thought one string of pearls would be best, rather than the usual three, as it would make for a more graphic look. Finally, I was given the opportunity to review The Queen's crowns in the Royal Collection next door and decided on one of the more relatively understated pieces – the Diadem – which features a simple cross. It is just sublime and is apparently one of Her Majesty's favourites, so seemingly a good choice.

On the day of the shoot, I got a call from one of the offices in the Palace to ask whether the crown was essential for the shoot. The President of the United States was staying at the time, so security was tight and the logistics of getting the Diadem to the shoot would be tricky. Something in me held firm. Yes, it was important. So Angela brought the piece over herself and told me that Her Majesty had said that if Chris wanted the Diadem, he must have the Diadem. Thank you, Your Majesty.

With the shoot well under way in the Yellow Drawing Room, I asked if we might have a change of cape, so Angela brought out the Ermine. Until the day I die, I will never forget the moment The Queen put it on – I felt I was somehow channelling the work. Her Majesty looked sensational – just beautiful – and the images we captured have become historic.

I'm proud of what we created together that day and I still have to pinch myself sometimes to remind myself that it wasn't a dream. The photoshoot was quite a surreal experience at times but I put my heart into the work and gave it my best. It was a huge honour and I'm grateful to Her Majesty for her faith in my art, to Jersey – the commissioning body – and to Angela for facilitating the work.'

By Chris Levine

Artist

'The experience of meeting and working with Angela and Her Majesty is a memory I treasure to this day. I was still a photographic assistant when I found myself in the surreal position of driving through the gates into the Buckingham Palace forecourt to meet The Queen for the first time back in 2003. Chris Levine was looking for an assistant to light Her Majesty for his holographic-portrait commission and I was the lucky lady who was hired. Shortly before we were due to go to the Palace for the first time, he also asked me to bring in my camera to document the making of the hologram and take some reference portrait shots.

What I remember most from that first meeting was how sparkly Her Majesty's eyes were and how beautiful her smile was, but more than that, I was overcome with the thought that she was very much like a grandmother – albeit a very famous one. I just wanted to go over and give her a big hug – totally against protocol, obviously. I felt bad that she was sitting in the middle of the room with all of us around her, almost like a goldfish being watched in a bowl. I remember saying just that to Angela, who suggested I go over and talk to her to break the ice and make me feel more comfortable: The Queen is famous for making everyone feel at ease. So I did. I believe I even told her that she reminded me of my own nonna at one point. I also remember – probably much to everyone's horror! – telling her that part of the process we were doing that day would be just like having her passport photograph taken, and Her Majesty looking at me not at all unkindly for my blunder and babbling!

I was amazed at how The Queen made us all feel so at ease, and just how sweet and gentle she was, although at the same time I was in awe of her obvious sovereignty. I also felt privileged to witness the tender connection and intimacy between Angela and Her Majesty, an almost mother–daughter type of bond, yet one with much reverence and respect on Angela's part. It was apparent to me that I had a one-off opportunity to capture something precious – and that was quite something.

We were fortunate enough to be given a second sitting early in 2004 and this time I had permission to bring in my small digital camera to further document my experience. It was in this visit that I decided to capture the truly unique little moments that made the experience, and Her Majesty, so magical and memorable for me. That was when I photographed Angela helping adjust The Queen's outfit for the camera – I wanted to capture their relationship – and Her Majesty putting on the Diadem in the mirror. I remember naively imagining that surely there must be a person in the Palace whose sole job it was to place the crown on Her Majesty's head! That moment, and the image I captured of it, humanised Her Majesty for me: I wanted to capture that while retaining her undeniable nobility.

'I'm honoured that I had the opportunity to meet The Queen and was able
to capture those few moments to which I imagine few of us have access. I will
treasure these memories for a lifetime.'

By Nina Duncan

Photographer

ON THE FROW: LONDON FASHION WEEK

Although The Queen doesn't consider herself to be a fashion icon, I am very aware that many people do. She is always on-trend, trendsetting, in fact, never puts a foot wrong when it comes to choosing the outfits she wears, and takes inspiration from the classic styles of Dior and Chanel. The Queen is humble, and her life is about her role. It is part of her job to look the part, and fashion helps. I've had to be mindful over the years that when Her Majesty makes a speech, the media's focus should always be on her words and their subject matter, rather than the colour of her dress or the style of her hat, which can be a little limiting in how creative I can be with the design. So when the opportunity arose for The Queen to attend London Fashion Week, I was thrilled: for once, we could embrace the occasion without worrying quite as much as we would for a State engagement or an official Royal visit, when strict criteria must be taken into account in the designing of Her Majesty's clothes.

The origins of The Queen's iconic appearance on the 'FROW' (the front row) at the 2018 London Fashion Week show came from an idea that I had several months before. I'm such a fan of the fashion world, and considering how much everyone loves The Queen's sense of style, I wondered if we could create an award to mark the effect she has had on the fashion industry over the years. I thought it might also be a great opportunity to support an up-and-coming British designer. When I suggested to The Queen an award to be called 'The Queen Elizabeth II Award for British Design' that could be presented for the first time at London Fashion Week by The Queen personally, she loved the idea. In subsequent years, the award would be presented by another member of the Royal Family. Later, Her Majesty described the award as her 'legacy to all those who have contributed to the British fashion industry'. Sam Cohen,

Opposite: The Queen sits with Anna Wintour and me at Richard Quinn's runway show during London Fashion Week in 2018. I'm wearing a beautiful dress kindly designed for me by Stewart Parvin.

Her Majesty's Private Secretary at the time and I immediately got in touch with Caroline Rush at the British Fashion Council to get the ball rolling. She was absolutely delighted to hear that Her Majesty would attend the show and recognise young British talent in this way. The only thing missing was the award, which Her Majesty kindly agreed that I would be in charge of designing. I think she knew that I would create something in keeping with her own taste.

Designing an award is quite unlike designing an outfit, as I soon came to discover. I wanted to use The Queen Elizabeth Rose as the main focus for the design, but there were many other factors to consider, too. The award needed to be light enough for Her Majesty to hold easily but not so light that it felt insubstantial for the winner. For the design of the Rose, I envisaged it as giving the impression of having been carved into the bark of a tree, a modern design but still natural in tone. In the end, it turned out perfectly. Her Majesty was pleased when she saw it, and was confident that she could carry it!

In the lead-up to the show, which was hosted by the British Fashion Council, we had to keep everything tightly under wraps. If the media knew what was happening beforehand, it would have been very difficult for Her Majesty to attend as they would have flocked to the venue. Only a handful of people knew of the plan that The Queen would be presenting the award to Richard Quinn. My assistant, Jackie, Private Secretary, Sam Cohen, and I went to 180 Strand to see the venue before the event and to meet with the organisers. We assessed the suggested route that Her Majesty would take once she was inside, and I made some changes to the planned programme so that the new generation of designers attending would have the opportunity to speak to The Queen about their creations.

On the day of the show, I arrived with The Queen, who was wearing an Angela Kelly outfit: the design was modern but inspired by Chanel, duck egg blue in colour, accompanied by a matching jacket decorated with aquamarine Swarovski crystals. We were taken to meet the New Generation designers, who, as they saw Her Majesty approaching, responded in utter amazement, not only to have the chance of seeing The Queen, but also having the chance to speak with her and share their designs. Afterwards everyone was asked to take their seats, which was our cue to take our positions. The media still had no idea that Her Majesty was about to walk into the room. I was later told by Stella, Jackie, and my great friend Michael Atmore, from Fairchild Publications, who flew over from NYC for London Fashion week, that they could hear the New Generation designers talking about how they just met The Queen and how they were still shocked. As The Queen walked in, there were audible gasps from every direction, followed swiftly by camera shutters going off at speed. After the

As The Queen walked in, there were audible gasps from every direction.

Mood board for designing The Queen Elizabeth II Award for British Design by Lucy Price.

Me and my friend Michael Atmore.

initial shock, there was a spontaneous round of applause and some of the media representatives even had tears in their eyes – it's so unusual for anyone to see The Queen in this way and everyone was thrilled to capture Her Majesty in this rare moment.

It was a personal privilege for me that day to be able to sit with The Queen on the front row alongside iconic figures in fashion such as Caroline Rush, Anna Wintour, Sarah Mower, and Anya Hindmarch. The show began and Her Majesty later told me that she particularly loved seeing all the florals on the catwalk. Afterwards, The Queen and I made our way to the front where she made a wonderful speech about the importance of British fashion. I shall never forget seeing The Queen presenting Richard Quinn with the inaugural Queen Elizabeth II Award for British Design.

Opposite: When Richard found out The Queen was there – he added head scarves at the last minute, a touch that The Queen appreciated.

Below: The Queen presents Richard Quinn the inaugural Queen Elizabeth II Award for British Design during London Fashion Week in 2018. What an honour to be on stage with The Queen, Caroline Rush, and Sarah Mower.

CHAPTER 4

On The Move

THE ROYAL TRAIN

We often travel across the country to engagements on the Royal Train. Although I can't disclose much about what happens on the train, I can give an idea of what a typical journey on it involves. And I can definitely tell you about the fun we have, especially if we're staying overnight somewhere. Travelling around the United Kingdom with The Queen in this way is a truly wonderful experience.

Before we leave Buckingham Palace, my team makes sure that everything is packed as efficiently as possible – as you can imagine, there isn't much space on the train for luggage. The train isn't as big as you might think as there are only six to eight coaches, depending on who is travelling with The Queen. All in all, there are only ever about twelve staff on board – Her Majesty never has a large entourage.

As soon as we board the train at the station, I get straight to work unpacking. Occasionally, when we are on longer trips, I may need to press a few items. It didn't take me long to learn that ironing on a moving train is almost like surfing! You just need to find your balance as the train rocks back and forth. And, as with the ironing, other work on the train isn't as straightforward or relaxing as it should be. Sadly, there isn't time to sit and watch the beautiful scenery go by, although I always catch a glimpse here and there as we head towards our destination, especially to the north, which is so familiar to me.

When we arrive at our destination, I ensure that The Queen has everything she needs for the day and make some final checks on her dress, coat, and hat, because as soon as she steps off the train, she will be greeted by press and photographers. Everything must be perfect. As Her Majesty steps onto the platform, my heart lifts when I hear cheering and applause, and see Union Jack flags waving in the crowds. The mayor of whichever town we are visiting usually comes to greet The Queen and, in the background, you often catch trainspotters making hurried notes about the unusual model they've just seen.

On one special occasion, about ten years ago, I even got to enjoy my very own warm welcome when the Royal Train stopped in Liverpool. All of my family – my children and grandchildren – came to the station to see me and we

Opposite: The Queen arrives at Runcorn by Royal Train in 2018.

hugged and kissed on the platform. I'm so glad I have pictures of that special moment: it was the first time my family had seen me on the Royal Train.

Even after The Queen has left for her engagement, there's no time to waste as I need to prepare for her return and pack everything if we're heading straight back to London. While we're waiting on board, it can be slightly unnerving when the train keeps reversing in and out of the station to allow commuter trains onto the platform – the Royal Train can never be in the way and must not disrupt others as they travel about the country. Her Majesty would hate to make anyone late. Although, saying this, the less time we spend on the platform the better, as far as I'm concerned! I do find it a little embarrassing when I'm taking a break from packing, and am preparing to sit in the dining car to eat something. People on the platform can see right in through the windows and you do start to feel like you're on display! Over the years, I have learned to close the curtains to save embarrassment all round.

I'm always planning ahead, so if we're going back to London that day I'll be thinking about what's next on the agenda, whether it's at the Palace or at Windsor Castle. Occasionally, though, I'll take a moment to look at people's faces as we pass through stations. It's lovely to see how much everyone appreciates seeing the Royal Train.

Miss Peggy Hoath on board the Royal Train in 1994.

The Queen and The
Duke of Edinburgh
arrive on the Royal
Train at Birmingham
New Street Station
in 2015.

BRITANNIA

During its decades of service, the magnificent *Britannia* was the setting for many
Royal engagements, and it was a wonderful way to travel. Whether on a formal
or private tour, the elegantly designed Royal Yacht offered a home-away-from-
home to The Queen and her family. I was privileged to join Her Majesty aboard
Britannia on several occasions, and although I'd like to describe the beauty of
the State Drawing Room, the Sun Lounge or the Admiral's Cabin, I'm afraid
I simply can't do them justice! I can, however, safely say that being on *Britannia*
was an amazing experience: it transported me to a world away from the hustle
and bustle of Buckingham Palace, and it was always so much more relaxed. The
minute Her Majesty came on board, anyone could tell she felt secure and at ease.
It didn't matter where we were going – from South Africa to Helsinki – *Britannia*
felt like home. Of course, The Queen is never truly on holiday as she still has
to meet with her Private Secretaries and work her way through the famous red
boxes, which still managed to reach Her Majesty even on *Britannia* – one of the
Royal Yacht's lifeboats would go to pick them up from the nearest port.

Of all the State occasions held on *Britannia*, one in particular will stay with
me for ever. It was 24 March 1995 and Her Majesty was due to watch the iconic
Beating of the Retreat in the harbour at Durban, in South Africa – a pageant
of music and military drills, fireworks and cannons – after hosting a State
Banquet for the great Nelson Mandela, followed by a reception for 200 guests.
I remember that The Queen was particularly excited about the dinner and was
very much looking forward to joining her guests when I was helping her get
ready. For this occasion, Her Majesty and I had decided on a beautiful soft pink
dress with a subtle pink lace overlay. As ever, it was a pleasure to see Her Majesty,
elegantly dressed and perfectly complementing the beautiful gowns and smart
suits of her guests, against the glorious backdrop of *Britannia*.

As the evening went on, I could hear music beginning to play and the gentle
hum of chatter and laughter. Safe in the knowledge that I'd finished my duties
for the day, I went back to my cabin and changed into my pyjamas. As I was
settling into my nightly routine, I suddenly heard my name being shouted from
the corridor. Slightly alarmed, I ran out of my cabin only to find Her Majesty
standing right in front of me. At first, I didn't know where to look, but almost

**Opposite: Royal Yacht
Britannia departing
Portsmouth in 2007.**

instantly, a broad smile broke across her face and I found myself grinning with her – our outfits, although very different, were exactly the same shade of soft pink. I was asked to follow Her Majesty to her cabin because she needed something before dinner, and once she was ready to join her guests again, I curtsied and said goodnight.

As The Queen walked away that evening, I was still quietly laughing to myself and certainly went to bed with a smile. It was one of many happy moments we shared on board *Britannia*. The Royal Yacht's crew were so diligent and considerate – we felt like one big happy family. Often when my evening duties were done, I would go outside and sit on a step and just watch the sea go by – at those times I always wished I had my telescope with me as the stars reflecting in the ocean were mesmerising.

I ran out of my cabin to find Her Majesty standing right in front of me.

The Queen and Nelson
Mandela in South
Africa in 1995.

THE QUEEN'S LUGGAGE

A huge amount of preparation is involved in getting everything ready for any travelling, and especially for a Royal Tour, from creating the outfits and matching the hats, to making sure the appropriate shoes, gloves, and handbags are selected and prepared. On a ten-day tour there might be up to thirty outfits for packing: this allows us to offer two outfits to choose from for each engagement, and if neither is quite right, or one gets soaking wet, we always have a backup. Sometimes we will pack two hats for each outfit – a lightweight one for warmer weather and a stronger, sturdier one in case it gets chilly or starts to rain. When everything has been readied, I ask for The Queen's Footmen to prepare the Royal luggage and deliver Her Majesty's to the Dressers' Floor, so that we can begin to pack it all.

Many aspects of my role have remained unchanged from when my predecessor, Peggy Hoath, was in charge. But, as with any job over the course of a quarter of a century, certain things eventually need changing or processes can be improved, and this is something I'm always mindful of. That was definitely the case when it came to Her Majesty's luggage.

Years ago, The Queen travelled with three very large, and very heavy, leather wardrobes. In fact, they were heavy even when completely empty, and although sturdy and strong, with three large metal locks, over time the leather had become so worn that the handles were starting to disintegrate – not ideal for the poor Footmen whose responsibility it was to carry them from place to place, and up and down stairs. There were three large wardrobes from the early years, plus a new, smaller, leather wardrobe that had been given to Her Majesty as a present by her children. Before each tour, these would be packed with The Queen's clothes and transported to the aeroplane, where they would stand upright in the hold, along with all the other luggage and cargo. Over the years, we tended to travel in smaller planes with less cargo space, as the length of the tours was condensed, with more engagements on each day, so the wardrobes

Opposite: Everything labelled and ready to go.

had to be laid flat and strapped to the floor inside the plane behind where we all sat. The airline was happy to help with this – even removing some seats to make space – but, as you can imagine, this was all becoming a bit of a nightmare: we constantly worried that The Queen's clothing might end up damaged and I'm sure the crew who unloaded the luggage dreaded our arrival.

I realised we couldn't possibly keep asking people to lift these wardrobes and

Saying farewell to the wonderful Milan.

cases any longer – it was getting ridiculous – so I had to come up with a better, more practical solution. My immediate thought was to use hanging bags instead and, at first, I was pleasantly surprised that this seemed to work quite well. When they were being packed, each hanging bag stored two outfits – a dress and a coat or jacket – the heavier items and the silk garments in separate bags to protect the more delicate materials. This change was met with huge relief by the Footmen and porters!

I seemed to have struck upon the perfect solution, until The Queen and The Duke of Edinburgh travelled to Italy in 2000. With all of Her Majesty's outfits packed in the correct bags and on the rail, ready to go, everything seemed to be going smoothly . . . until we arrived to a torrential downpour. The crew began unloading the luggage and someone decided to roll the rail of The Queen's hanging bags straight across the tarmac in the pouring rain. A huge gust of wind took hold and sent the bags flying across the ground, getting drenched by the rain. I watched the whole thing happen in slow motion from a window in the plane – I felt so sorry for them scrambling around trying to pick up Her Majesty's soaked clothes. Of course, we made sure that that never happened again, and I began straight away to think up another solution to this very old problem.

Another aspect of my role is to look after The Queen's personal Royal Warrants. They are issued to companies and individuals who are asked to supply personal goods to The Queen, from shoes to handbags and much more. To maintain a Royal Warrant, a company must demonstrate excellent service, not just to The Queen but to the general public, so from time to time I will go to visit them to check that their members of staff are treating their customers with respect. One company with a Royal Warrant is House of Fraser, so I decided to go for a browse to see if they might have anything suitable in the way of luggage. I soon found the solution: suitcases with wheels! I bought quite a few lightweight Linea cases, once again to the delight of the Buckingham Palace staff members who had risked their backs each time we went on tour. I'm happy to say that this has been a successful and very welcome change.

When it comes to packing the new, lightweight (and waterproof!) cases, our approach is meticulous to ensure that there is no creasing or damaging of Her Majesty's clothes. It is important to balance the weight on each side of the case and, whenever possible, to start with heavier items, or those made of hardier material, at the bottom. You may not know that tissue paper is an invaluable tool in the packing of The Queen's luggage: we use layers of it to separate and protect individual items, from jumpers and cardigans all the way up to stocks and socks. We also use plenty of tissue paper to protect Her Majesty's hats in their boxes, and although I still use hanging bags and the rail for some outfits, we're all extremely careful if the weather isn't pleasant that day!

THE SPECIAL ESCORT GROUP – AT YOUR SERVICE, MA'AM

Imagine standing outside the gates at Buckingham Palace and seeing a row of white police motorcycles lined up on the forecourt. Behind them, there is a set of black doors, and behind these doors two cars wait. We are about to leave Buckingham Palace on our way to the airport. The last pieces of luggage are packed into the boots of the cars, and I have The Queen's personal luggage next to me on the seat. In the car with me are the chauffeur and The Queen's Footman, Ian Robinson. We are parked at the Garden Entrance waiting for Her Majesty The Queen to appear, with an additional car for members of the Royal Household, such as the Ladies-in-Waiting, the Private Secretary and The Queen's Equerry. We are all to drive to the airport at the same time in convoy.

Every day The Queen's programme runs like clockwork. We always set off at the exact time stated in it. My excitement – after twenty-five years I'm still excited! starts as the big black doors open at the side of Buckingham Palace and you can see the public outside waiting. They have no idea who is in the car driving out through those black doors, but as it gets nearer you can see their faces change with astonishment when they realise it is The Queen. Then they start to cheer.

Four police motorcyclists from the Special Escort Group (SEG) wait for us to come through the gates and join us, one at the front of the convoy leading the way, and three others who deal with the traffic and clear the route for us. They will ensure that The Queen gets to her destination safely and on time. On this particular occasion we are driving along The Mall towards Marble Arch. The SEG will stop other cars to allow The Queen's and those behind it in the convoy to pass through the traffic faster. They do not hold up the traffic for more than a minute or so. Once we pass the first bike, the other three speed off, blowing their

Opposite: It's always thrilling to see people's faces as The Queen drives past.

Right: The Queen
and The Prince of
Wales travel from
Buckingham Palace
to the Houses of
Parliament.

Below: *Vulcan, the
new recruit.*

whistles to get attention (they don't use sirens) and we move swiftly on to the next junction where the SEG bikes wait for us to pass, then zoom off to stop the traffic ahead so we have a clear run. It is like playing leapfrog. A police Range Rover travels behind our cars making sure no one gets too close.

As we pass members of the public, who have stopped to see what is going on, people cheer and clap when they see the car driving by and realise The Queen is sitting inside. 'It's The Queen! It's The Queen!' And as everyone seems to have a smartphone these days, they try to get a photograph or a video of Her Majesty's escort passing. If The Queen happens to catch someone's eye, she will wave, of course. Imagine how busy the streets of London can be: our escort has to make their way down some narrow streets. The SEG are so professional and have to be precise when moving in and out of traffic, keeping it clear for The Queen to get to her destination without holding up the traffic for too long. It is fascinating to watch them manoeuvre so rapidly, with excellent communication between them. The Queen will use the SEG as escorts only when there is an official engagement, or in an emergency.

When I'm travelling in a convoy like this, I cannot help but smile at how happy the public are to see The Queen and how lucky I am to be travelling just a few cars behind Her Majesty.

*'It's The Queen!
It's The Queen!'*

CHAPTER 5

The Eyes of the World

WOMAN TO WOMAN

When I am designing for The Queen, I am always aware of how her outfits will be perceived, both by the people she is meeting with or speaking to, as well as by the media. However, just as eyes are always on Her Majesty, they are often also on the people she interacts with, and there is much speculation about how one is meant to behave.

Contrary to what many people believe, there are no strict rules that must be followed when one is introduced to The Queen. You may wish, or not wish, to curtsey. But on the whole most people do curtsey or bow out of respect. Some women tend to find that they instinctively curtsey, whereas men tend to bow, but there is no golden rule, even for the most long-standing members of the Royal Household. Each morning and evening, I greet Her Majesty with a curtsey, but because I see her so often, I don't repeat the gesture throughout the day unless we are out in public on Tour.

There are certain things that are understood to be accepted protocol when it comes to interacting with Her Majesty, though. Supposedly, you should never put your arm around The Queen, for example, but when human instincts kick in, sometimes this is absolutely the appropriate thing to do. The Queen has the ability to make everyone feel so relaxed that sometimes it feels instinctive to be tactile with her, just as Michelle Obama demonstrated during the State Visit with her husband, President Obama, in 2009.

Much has been made about the meeting between Michelle and Her Majesty, when an instant and mutual warmth was shared between these two remarkable women, and protocol was seemingly 'abandoned' as they stood closely with their arms around each other's' backs. In reality, it was a natural instinct for The Queen to show affection and respect for another great woman, and really there is no protocol that must be adhered to. When fondness is felt or the host of a State Visit goes to guide Her Majesty up some steps, it truly is about human kindness, and this is something The Queen will always welcome warmly. Anyone who is close to Her Majesty is not a threat and is certainly trusted.

Most people bow or curtsey out of respect, but there is no golden rule

Opposite: The Queen and Michelle Obama at Buckingham Palace in 2009.

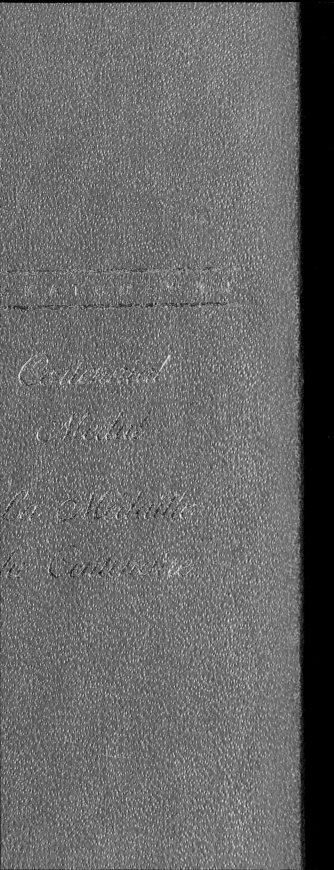

A PERSONAL HONOUR

I never know what will land on my desk each day. It might be a specific request from a photographer for a photoshoot, or for Her Majesty to take part in a spoof James Bond film! I have fond memories of one request in particular, which came to me via the Private Secretary's office in 2005 from the sculptor Susan Velder, who had been commissioned by the province of Saskatchewan to create something to mark the fiftieth anniversary of The Queen's reign, which was to be presented to Her Majesty on her visit to Canada later that year.

Susan had been commissioned to create a life-size statue of Her Majesty in bronze and it was to depict The Queen riding her favourite horse, Burmese, which was given to Her Majesty by the Royal Canadian Mounted Police and which she rode for eighteen consecutive years on her birthday parade, also known as Trooping the Colour. Her Majesty has always ridden side-saddle on that occasion, and as she is Colonel-in-Chief, she wears the full Guards' regiment uniform as well as a tricorn hat. The biretta, as it is also known, is a square cap with three flat projections on top – it's quite a tricky one to design correctly in fabric, let alone in bronze, as Susan came to discover.

Susan got in touch because, although things were going well with her designing of Burmese, The Queen and her uniform, she was struggling with the tricorn hat, finding it difficult to capture the fibres, the shape and the size. As you can imagine, a life-size bronze statue is no easy feat by any means, so to think that the hat was causing her so much trouble is quite something! She asked if I could provide a photograph of the biretta to help her.

Knowing how important this request was, and the significance of the statue to the people of Saskatchewan, I was determined to help as much as I could. The sculpture needed to be ready for the Royal Tour later that year and, as luck would have it, I was due to go on the usual recce to Canada in the not-too-distant future. Rather than sending a photo, which I worried wouldn't be helpful enough, I asked The Queen if I could take the actual hat with me on the recce, deliver it to Susan and leave it with her. When we arrived on the Royal visit later, I could collect it and all would be well. Her Majesty, as ever, was happy to help,

Opposite: *An unexpected honour.*

even though this was such an unusual request, and when I let Susan know my plan, she was thrilled.

So, three months later, we arrived at Saskatchewan for the unveiling of the statue and everything went exactly according to plan. The statue was enthusiastically received, the hat looked great, and Her Majesty was delighted. However, the night before we were due to move on to our next engagement, I received a request to be in the Audience Room of Government House the next morning at 11am. I went to sleep that night slightly perturbed, wondering what this was all about.

The next morning, I walked into the Audience Room to find that many chairs had been set out. To me, it looked like an Investiture and to my astonishment, I noticed that one of the chairs had my name on it. Still uncertain about what was happening, I sat down. Everyone else arrived shortly afterwards, and when we were all seated, Lieutenant Governor Lynda Haverstock called my name. In shock, I stood up and made my way to the stage where I was presented with the Saskatchewan Order of Merit medal for my help with Susan's work. I couldn't believe it! I was so proud and honoured that I cried when I received this special award. Sobbing as I returned to my seat, I knew from then on that Saskatchewan would always remain in my heart.

Spare time in Canada.

Notice the fibres and details on the hat which were hard to recreate in bronze, and why Susan needed to see the hat in person to help perfect the statue.

Susan Velder's sculpture.

SCARLETT THE YOUNG DESIGNER

I've no doubt that my love for fashion and my lifelong fascination with fabrics and design came from my mum. After all, I was surrounded by it as a child – our back room was a hive of dressmaking activity and, especially when I was in my early teens, I rarely saw my mum away from her Singer sewing machine, and so I had a strong instinct for dressmaking. In turn, I have shared my passion with my granddaughter, Scarlett, and I swear she has an instinct for fashion. She's a natural. It must run in the family.

Scarlett has lots of interests, including football, painting, and drawing, as well as making up her own fantasy characters, but she always takes a keen interest in my work. From when she was tiny, I've brought material samples home to show her, and now we talk about how thickness and texture affect the design of an outfit, which colours work well together, and how to create something spectacular for a special occasion.

Scarlett was four when I was planning for the 2010 Royal Tour to Canada, and I was thinking in particular about what Her Majesty might wear for the Canada Day celebrations she would attend. Scarlett was asking all the right questions straight away – would it be warm or cool? Who else would be there? It would be a formal occasion, I told her, with many members of the military, who would be wearing their fine red tunics, and I showed her a picture of the Canadian flag. Scarlett took in all of the information – she's always keen to learn – and then she let me know some of her own ideas on the direction I should take.

The Queen's outfit should be red and white, she said confidently, so I showed her some possible options for the material. She picked a smart but relatively lightweight fabric: perfect for the weather conditions. Then, she came up with the brilliant idea of including two extra layers on the dress – a sort of large frill that wrapped twice around from the hip, which would move very elegantly as Her Majesty walked. The hat, she thought, should be white and decorated with a large red flower. I thought all of these were lovely ideas and promised Scarlett

Opposite: The Queen in Ottawa on Canada Day in 2001, wearing the iconic Canadian Maple Leaf Royal Brooch. It was bought by King George VI for The Queen Mother in 1939 on what was the first ever State Visit by a reigning monarch.

I would stick to her design. True to my word, when I went back to London I brought Scarlett's vision to life in the workroom. Scarlett, of course, saw nothing unusual in this: she thought she was just helping her granny.

And then, at the celebrations on Canada Day, I felt so proud to watch The Queen wearing an outfit inspired by my granddaughter's creativity.

Considering how brilliantly the Canada Day outfit had gone down with everyone – Her Majesty and the media included – I was thrilled when on Scarlett's most recent visit, in 2019, when she was thirteen, she wanted to help again. I had a dress of The Queen's that she had worn quite often to private dinners which was in need of a revamp. I intended to adjust its length but to do this I needed to remove the delicate black beading from around the gown's lace hem. Without hesitation, Scarlett got on with the job, carefully unpicking it so that we could reuse the beading and lace on another part of the dress. She really is an excellent assistant, and probably far more patient than I am! I love sharing my passion with my granddaughter and I can't wait to see what life has in store for her.

Below: *Scarlett working on The Queen's evening dress at my cottage.*

Opposite: *The Queen inspects a Guard of Honour outside Canadian Parliament on Canada Day celebrations in 2010.*

A FITTING TRIBUTE

A Royal Tour, for the people who come to greet The Queen, and the British media, who often travel great distances to report on her travels, is always a special event. As such, when designing Her Majesty's outfits for these occasions, I'm always looking to introduce a significant detail – ideally something that acknowledges or reflects the location of her visit.

During the 2010 Canadian tour, Her Majesty and Prince Philip were due to attend a State Banquet in Toronto to celebrate Canada Day. For such a special occasion, I wanted to design something as a tribute to the country. So having chosen a white dress that was fitted but also comfortable for The Queen to walk in, I decided to add some detail that made use of the maple leaf – the most recognised symbol of Canada. Each leaf has eleven points and I wanted to make sure that this was reflected in the design of the dress. I managed to find a beautiful lacquered print material in white, which I thought would be well suited to appliqué, and worked up a design that featured maple leaves running down the right shoulder and arm of the dress. The leaves were to be produced in Swarovski crystals to complement the simplicity of the gown. When I showed my design to The Queen, she agreed that this was a lovely idea.

Canada was such a distance for the British media to travel to and I knew that some reporters and photographers were due to fly back before the banquet and wouldn't see the maple-leaf outfit. Although it had never been done before, and has never been done since, I decided to ask The Queen if she would grant special permission for some of the media to have access to the dress before the event itself. Her Majesty was happy to help, considering the long distance they had travelled, so the day before the banquet, Judy Wade, the Royal Correspondent for *Hello!* magazine, and her photographer John Stillwell came to meet me in Government House, where we were staying. The staff there were kind enough to arrange a room with lovely natural light for the photographs to be taken. I positioned the dress in the sunlight and John was able to capture the sparkle of the crystals. The results

Opposite: The Queen gives a speech in Toronto in 2010. 'The Girls of Great Britain and Ireland' Tiara is one of the lightest of the tiaras, which is why The Queen wears it so often.

were sensational – the image was featured on the front cover of *Hello!*, Judy and John were thrilled to have been given the opportunity and to have secured the best shots for their magazine, and I was pleased to have been able to help.

When The Queen was seen in the maple leaf dress the following evening at the State Banquet, the media went wild. Everyone loved the design and that the leaves all had the correct number of points – attention to detail always goes down well. It is at moments like that that I feel truly privileged to design dresses for Her Majesty's special occasions, and for the media to capture and acknowledge my work gives me reassurance and the confidence to keep designing for the next event, wherever and whenever that may be!

The intricate detailing of the Maple Leaf dress – this is when attention to detail really matters!

**The Queen and The
Duke of Edinburgh at a
State Dinner in Toronto
in 2010.**

PEOPLE OF THE DAWN

As part of the same 2010 Royal Tour to Canada, The Queen was scheduled to travel to Halifax, Nova Scotia, for a meeting with members of the local First Nations Mi'kmaq tribe, also known as the 'People of the Dawn'. As always, I had been on a recce some months before to familiarise myself and others with the programme of events. Recces always mean long days of work, ensuring that everything is in order and that we are preparing and planning for any eventuality, but they are certainly worth it for the peace of mind they offer. They usually take three or four days, with the Private Secretary leading the small team. I go mostly to plan the accommodation needs, working with the Private Secretary on the timing of the engagements. On that occasion, I had the privilege of a personal meeting with the Mi'kmaqs and their chief.

In preparation, I'd been researching the customs of the tribe. Much of their traditional clothing was adorned with the most elaborate and beautiful beadwork – I couldn't even imagine the precision and skill involved in such detailed work. It provided me with inspiration for the outfit I was designing for Her Majesty to wear at their meeting. I had in mind a beautiful canary yellow material that would make a gorgeous jacket and skirt, but I wanted it to be embellished in such a way that would pay tribute to the traditions and hospitality of the Mi'kmaq people. So when I was finally introduced to their chief, I asked whether he and his tribe would be so kind as to design something for the collar and cuffs of Her Majesty's outfit. Of course, I would give free rein in terms of design and the colouring of the beads – theirs is a tradition that goes back hundreds of years, and it was an honour to incorporate some of their work in one of my own creations. I explained that the material would be sent to them from the British Embassy, and the Mi'kmaqs said they would be happy to help.

Back in London, I was excited when a parcel arrived a few months later containing the completed cuffs and collar. The craftsmanship was exquisite and so beautiful. I'm used to working with embellishments and know most of the tricks of the trade: keep in mind the fabric with which you're working – heavier beads won't work on lighter, chiffon-style fabrics; sequins and crystals require

Opposite: The Queen attends a reception for celebrating Nova Scotia in 2010.

someone with perfect eyesight to stitch them on as it's such a delicate and painstaking job. It can take many days to achieve the desired result, but at the end, it's satisfying to know that you have produced something truly unique. The work of the Mi'kmaq tribe was some of the loveliest I have ever seen.

On the day of the engagement, Her Majesty was delighted to meet the Mi'kmaq community and the ladies who had helped create her outfit. I will never forget the pride on their faces.

This beading detail is so beautiful.

THE SNOW QUEEN

When I'm preparing for one of Her Majesty's Royal Tours, one of the first things I consider, along with any cultural sensitivities, is the predicted weather conditions of the hosting country. The Queen's outfits must be made of the right material so that she is comfortable when completing her engagements: no one likes to be dressed for the wrong weather!

In 2008, Her Majesty was invited to Slovenia and Slovakia for a four-day State Visit. Three months before, I travelled with a small group of the Royal Household to both countries to do our usual recce ahead of the Royal visit. The weather was warm when we were there, as it was midsummer, but I was told there was a good chance of snow at the time of Her Majesty's visit. Immediately I felt inspired: it was my first chance to design a winter wonderland wardrobe for The Queen. As we went about our recce, colours, shapes, and styles were leaping into my head: hats, silk jersey dresses, and stunning evening gowns. Her Majesty needed to look glamorous on every occasion: there must not be a 'stand-out' outfit that overshadowed the rest, especially since she would be visiting two countries. There were also cultural sensitivities to take into account: would any particular colour be considered offensive or inappropriate?

Full of ideas, I returned to London and began creating. All outfits for important engagements are created from scratch. I knew that Her Majesty would be attending a State Banquet in Slovenia, to be hosted by the President, and I immediately thought of the perfect material to use for this occasion. The Queen needed a long evening dress; I knew there was some beautiful brocade in the cupboard, wrapped in black tissue paper to preserve its fine silver thread. It had been there for decades – possibly as long as forty years – and it's quite a moment when you unwrap a parcel like this: a gift made to The Queen long ago, kept carefully in the cupboard until the right time comes to use it. Its pale blue and silver colourings would perfectly complement the wintry setting of the banquet.

Although I give all of Her Majesty's outfits the same care and consideration, another event was scheduled on this tour for which I was particularly excited to design something. The Queen and The Duke of Edinburgh were due to

Opposite: The Queen attends a State Banquet at Brdo Castle during a State Visit to Slovenia in 2008.

visit Starý Smokovec via a funicular railway to the peak of Hrebienok, where they would unveil a plaque to mark a wheelchair-accessible tourist pathway called 'Tatras Without Barriers'. It was a lovely engagement: with the path, the less physically able would be enabled to visit this beautiful spot. Given that they would be travelling high into the Slovakian Tatras mountains, I knew Her Majesty's outfit had to be warm but I wanted to design something that complemented the weather conditions, should it be snowing. I decided on an off-white wool tweed coat, trimmed with fur on the collar and cuffs for extra insulation, and a matching dress of the same material, from which I also asked Stella McLaren to make a matching hat. For decoration, we chose feathers and sequins, which would sparkle, hopefully through the falling snow.

When we arrived in Slovakia, it was unusually warm for the time of year, but I had packed a pair of comfortable but stylish black boots for The Queen – they would be perfect for snowy conditions.

That morning, I was praying for snow, and as Her Majesty and His Royal Highness journeyed up the mountain on the train, sure enough it started to fall. It was the most magical sight – a crisp white blanket slowly settling all around. The Queen donned the stylish black boots I'd packed just in case, and the press went wild as she'd never been seen in anything like it before. In fact, Her Majesty was quite the trendsetter on that occasion, and when I think back to that moment, I can't help but think: Snow Queen.

The mink trim on this dress has now been removed and will be replaced with fake fur.

Opposite: *These boots were meant for walking! The Queen and the President of Slovakia, Ivan Gasparovic tour Hrebienok Ski Resort.*

TIME IS OF
THE ESSENCE

Despite hours, days, or even weeks of preparation for any Royal engagement, there are occasions that require quick thinking from my team and even sometimes The Queen herself. On those days when Her Majesty requires a last-minute alteration or a swift change of garment or accessory, I'm often reminded of a visit to Abu Dhabi.

In September 2010, roughly two months before The Queen and The Duke of Edinburgh were to spend five days in the Gulf Arab states, I went on the usual recce to familiarise myself with the setting and climate, as well as the route to and location of her engagements. As part of the Royal Tour, Her Majesty was due to visit the Sheikh Zayed Grand Mosque – one of the most beautifully decorated buildings I have ever seen. On my arrival, I was greeted by the local ladies who were to show me around. Walking quietly through the mosque, I felt calm and a sense of peace.

During my walkabout with the ladies, we decided there would be a small privacy screen where The Queen would change from her shoes into her socks and put on her longer coat, in keeping with the required dress code. Another screen would be set up in the area where she would be leaving the mosque, so that she could change back, just as she had when she had visited the mosque in the old Lincolnshire town of Scunthorpe in 2002, as part of the Golden Jubilee celebrations. Her Majesty is always more than happy to respect the customs of the sites and places she visits. In fact, she is a stickler for abiding by what is accepted or what is required.

In my experience, recces often provide inspiration when I'm designing the outfits to be worn by Her Majesty on a visit. The Grand Mosque in Abu Dhabi was so impressive that I quickly knew how to create something that would complement the grand setting. Dazzling crystal chandeliers hung from the ceiling, reflecting every colour of the rainbow, and beautiful patterns reminiscent of the Tree of Life adorned each pillar in red, blue and gold. I decided that The Queen should wear a long gold coat adorned with the same pattern, and I remembered that in the material stockroom at Buckingham Palace there was

Opposite: The Queen visits the Sheikh Zayed Grand Mosque in Abu Dhabi in 2010. Note the beading detail, which was specially obtained for this occasion and is reminiscent of the Tree of Life detailing inside the Mosque.

some very old golden material that had been presented to The Queen when she was still a princess. I knew it was in excellent condition and would be perfect for this occasion, although sadly I never discovered who gave it to her: records weren't kept before I started working at the Palace.

I shared my thoughts on the outfit with my guides and they were more than willing to help me bring my vision to life. The next day, they took me to the local indoor market, where I was introduced to a gentleman who created the most wonderful colourful beading I have ever seen – which is saying something, given the nature of my profession! Explaining my idea, the ladies asked if he would help by creating beading that matched the colours of the Tree of Life, which I would then use to decorate a long golden coat for Her Majesty to wear. He was very happy to help and was even content to be sworn to secrecy, even though he didn't know who he was working for. With all of The Queen's outfits, it's important that we keep everything top secret. Having arranged for the ladies to collect the beading and post it to me in London, I returned from that recce knowing this would be a very special outfit and hoping it would turn out to be worthy of the grand setting of the mosque.

Back in London, I set about bringing my creation to life. I had retrieved the golden material from the stockroom and I was safe in the knowledge that the beading was on its way, but I needed to consider what The Queen would wear as a headdress. Her Majesty would arrive for the engagement in a pillbox hat with gold corded trim and would travel straight to the mosque: I decided to add fasteners to the top of the hat and the shoulders of the coat: this would allow us to fix a scarf securely to the hat and for it to cross over The Queen's shoulders. This felt a fitting and practical solution to the problem, and while I was thinking of an appropriate scarf to use, I remembered I already owned just the thing! My sister, Donna, had given me a beautiful gold scarf years before and, as I had never worn it, I gave it to Her Majesty. When she considered the new owner of her gift, I knew Donna wouldn't mind – although I never did tell her or The Queen!

With the outfit in place, I had one final challenge to address: how would Her Majesty carry the longer coat, scarf and her white ankle socks to be worn

only when she arrived at the mosque?
Often my job requires creative
thinking – it's one of the things I
enjoy best about it – and I came up
with the solution of designing and
making a large cream canvas handbag
with detailed patterning. On the day,
the extra items of clothing would be
neatly folded and kept inside, ready
for Her Majesty to change into. With
all outfit preparations complete, I
was very much looking forward to
returning to Abu Dhabi and was
expecting a smooth, hiccup-free visit.
However, as I've discovered over my
years of service, you can't plan for
every potential hitch . . .

A few months later, The Queen's
convoy was on its way to the mosque and I was travelling with The Duke of
Edinburgh's valet a few cars back, just as we always do. The plan was in place:
the valet and I would go straight to the screened areas to help Her Majesty and
His Royal Highness to change into their outfits. However, as we approached
the mosque, the police allowed The Queen's car, and the escort to proceed, but
refused to let us in. We tried desperately to explain that it was crucial for us to be
allowed in, but we weren't understood and, after we'd spoken to Her Majesty's
driver on the phone, I knew that she was wondering where we were. Thankfully
we were finally allowed through. Although, in that instance, keeping calm and
carrying on just didn't do it for me!

Rushing to the screened area, I found Her Majesty and the relief on both
of our faces was priceless. We had to move quickly and, after I'd removed the
contents from the canvas bag, it became clear that the scarf was going to be a
problem. Given that we'd lost so much time, after changing into her white socks
and putting on the golden coat, Her Majesty had no time to fasten the scarf
as intricately as planned. The Duke of Edinburgh came to alert her that she
needed to join him immediately and, in need of a quick solution, Her Majesty
calmly draped the scarf over her hat, and her shoulders, loosely tied it under her
chin and off she went, right on time. Of course, she still looked amazing. The
Queen and I had worked together in a stressful moment to ensure that she could
continue with her important engagement.

'PRESIDENT AND FRIENDS'

When it comes to designing the outfits for Her Majesty's State Visits abroad, inspiration comes easier with some than with others. In May 2011, The Queen was due to travel to the Republic of Ireland. It was a particularly significant occasion: Her Majesty would be the first British Monarch to visit the country since 1911, when King George V, her grandfather, had made a tour and all of Ireland was still part of the United Kingdom. The highlight of the programme was to be a State Banquet, hosted by the Irish President, Mary McAleese, held in Dublin Castle, and I had a clear vision for the perfect dress.

The Queen and I discussed the possible design at length, and I explained that for this evening gown it might be nice to incorporate the shamrock, both as a sign of respect and because it is a famous lucky charm. Her Majesty thought that an abundance of shamrocks all over the bodice of her outfit would be a lovely gesture. In addition, I thought it would be charming to introduce the traditional Irish symbol of the harp. On State engagements, it is usually the Royal Family Orders that are worn on the left shoulder, but on this occasion we could make a change and agreed that an Irish harp made of Swarovski crystals would take their place. Since the banquet, we have actually had several enquiries asking if the 'harp brooch' would be going on display, but it is actually sewn onto the dress and I'm afraid it cannot be removed!

Finally, we had to decide on an appropriate tiara. I knew the public wanted to see Her Majesty in her finery, so I chose the 'Girls of Great Britain and Ireland' Tiara, which was given to Queen Mary, The Queen's grandmother, on her marriage in 1893 and then to The Queen as a wedding present. Her Majesty often wears it and I thought it would suit the occasion, especially since its silhouette looks like a row of girls from Britain and Ireland holding hands.

As is often the case, the execution of the idea proved to be much more time-consuming and intricate than I'd imagined. To apply 2,000 shamrocks to the bodice of Her Majesty's dress, Tina in my team first had to create a template, using a digital sewing machine, then each shamrock was individually hand-stitched on. It was painstaking work, but of course, we always do whatever we

Opposite: The Queen speaks to guests at a State dinner in Saint Patrick's Hall at Dublin Castle in 2011.

need to do to get the job done. We also had to pay great attention when it came to introducing the Irish harp made of Swarovski crystals to the left shoulder, as Guinness, the famous stout producers, also use this symbol as their logo. While the harp was being made, I kept checking, over and over again, to make sure that we hadn't got it wrong! I know Her Majesty would not have been impressed if she had ended up sporting the Guinness logo on her shoulder, especially given her reaction to a new hairstyle I'd tried a few months earlier.

On that occasion I'd decided to stay blonde on top but go dark underneath, which was a fashion trend at the time. When The Queen saw me the following morning, she looked at me and asked, 'Have you ever seen a pint of Guinness?' I replied that, yes, I had, and her response was simply, 'Hmm,' as if to say, 'I will say no more.' Needless to say, I was straight down to the hairdresser the next day to change it back to blonde.

On the evening of the banquet at Dublin Castle, as The Queen entered the room, everyone stood as she walked to give her speech. Her dress looked phenomenal and I knew she loved the intricate shamrock detail. After the guests took their seats, Her Majesty began to speak and, as a total surprise to everyone except the Private Secretary, she greeted the President, ladies and gentlemen in perfect Irish Gaelic: 'A Uachtaráin agus a chairde,' meaning 'President and friends'. The whole room was awestruck and you could even hear a few guests exclaiming, 'Wow!' A massive round of applause followed. I had never seen such admiration, and I couldn't help but think the shamrocks on The Queen's dress had brought magic or luck to that significant event.

The harp design (above) had to be clearly the Irish harp, and definitely not the Guinness one – which sits to the other side. The green shamrock (left) is hidden secretly on this dress.

INSPIRATION IS EVERYWHERE

As part of The Queen's extensive 2012 Diamond Jubilee Tour, she was due to visit Northern Ireland for two busy days of engagements. For this trip, I had two outfits to design: one for a Service of Thanksgiving in Enniskillen, County Fermanagh, after which Her Majesty and The Duke of Edinburgh would be attending St Michael's Catholic church. This would be The Queen's first visit to a Catholic church in Northern Ireland, so it would be an historic moment. The second outfit was for Her Majesty to wear while she and His Royal Highness travelled around the Stormont Parliament Buildings while standing in an open-top car.

When I learned about the Service of Thanksgiving, I knew immediately what colour I would suggest for Her Majesty to wear. Given that she had worn green on her recent visit to the Republic of Ireland, I wanted her to wear something different for her first day of the trip and I had the perfect material in the stockroom – a beautiful pale blue. I've always found it fascinating that different colours can symbolise certain emotions or moods, and this soft hue seemed particularly fitting for the occasion. But I needed some additional design elements to bring the outfit to life. As always seems to be the way, I found inspiration in front of my eyes when I was walking through the corridors of Windsor Castle and noticed a beautiful Wedgwood collection. The china was exactly the same colour as the blue material I'd selected, and I decided to recreate its delicate pattern in fine lace for Her Majesty's dress and hat.

Surely no one can visit the Emerald Isle without wearing some green, so for The Queen's second outfit I settled on a lime fabric. Knowing that there would be lots of crowds and commotion as Her Majesty and His Royal Highness drove around the Parliament Buildings, I wanted her to stand out in a vibrant colour. Everyone must be able to catch a glimpse of Her Majesty when they've come out especially to see her! I also wanted to soften the outfit ever so slightly and decided to introduce some gold lace detailing to the unusual double collar of the jacket, as well as to the hat. Finally, I thought a single gold feather placed diagonally across the front of the hat would bring everything together nicely.

Opposite: The Queen visits a hospital in Enniskillen in Northern Ireland.

The visit to Northern Ireland went brilliantly and Her Majesty's outfits were well received. At both engagements, The Queen looked elegant and stylish, and I think she was pleased with her reception by the crowds and the media. The following year, I received a request from Hillsborough Castle, the official Royal Residence in Belfast, asking if the blue and lime green pieces might be included in an exhibition, as well as the outfits that The Queen had worn on her visit to the Republic of Ireland. As well as my own designs, an outfit created by the late Karl Ludwig – a previous designer for Her Majesty – would be featuring. I'm always eager to enable as many people as possible to get a close look at Her Majesty's clothes, so we were very happy to oblige.

The Wedgewood-inspired outfit in all its glory.

Opposite: The Queen and The Duke of Edinburgh drive in an open-top car in the grounds of the Stormont Estate in Belfast in 2012.

Above and left: *The Queen wears a lot of green – and I wanted to give another take here. Using gold lace on the hat and collar, and the gold feather – something a little different – Her Majesty is still clearly visible among the colourful crowds.*

THE WHITE HOUSE

As the world's longest-reigning monarch, The Queen has met many Presidents of the United States. However, there was a moment on her fifth visit to the country in 2007 that will stay with me for ever: a true reminder of the joys of my job and just how fortunate I am to work so closely with Her Majesty.

It was May – a lovely warm time of year in the United States – and Her Majesty and The Duke of Edinburgh had been invited by President George W. Bush to visit the White House as part of a Royal Tour of the country. The Queen and The Duke were first due to travel to Virginia, the site of the first permanent English settlement, at Jamestown, in America, before attending the famous Kentucky Derby in Louisville. On their arrival at the White House, a State ceremony on the South Lawn had been arranged, which would be attended by thousands of people, and later that evening, the President was to host the first white-tie dinner of his presidency in honour of the occasion. I had never been to Washington before and I was invited, along with other members of the Royal Household, to have dinner in the Map Room – I knew I'd be pinching myself throughout the experience!

As always with a Royal Tour, I had lots of things to consider and many outfits to create. But on this occasion, I was thinking a lot about one engagement in particular: the ceremony on the South Lawn, for which The Queen was to arrive directly from the White House. I kept thinking about the brightness of the famous building, and what an amazing backdrop it would make for whichever outfit Her Majesty wore. I knew that it had to complement this setting perfectly, particularly as she would be making a speech in front of thousands of guests.

With this upcoming visit I wanted something different for the event. After considering many options – different colour combinations, different styles of hat, different cuts and materials – I knew exactly how to showcase Her Majesty's elegance and pay tribute to the occasion. Against the brilliance of the White House walls, only a simple but stylish black and white outfit would do, although to my knowledge she'd never worn a monochrome outfit before. I remember

Opposite: The Queen with President George Bush at the White House in 2007. The black lace was placed over the crown of her hat, and then adorned with the black and white flower.

thinking, with a white jacket and a black lace collar, it could work! I also thought a white hat covered with the same black lace could look the part. So as part of my preparations for the tour, I excitedly set about finding the perfect material – a lightweight waffle weave – and sketching the shape of the white jacket with black lace detail shaped around the neckline in a scalloped effect.

On the day of the ceremony, I remember so clearly watching Her Majesty step out from the grand White House and greet the cheerful crowds alongside the President, The Duke of Edinburgh, and the President's wife, Laura. As America's First Lady, I am certain the pressure of looking the part was immense for Mrs Bush, too. But The Queen looked so lovely that day – I just watched and could hardly believe what I'd achieved. The Queen stood out in that iconic dress in front of that iconic building. I never normally take in a moment like that one because I have work to do – the next thing to consider, something else to prepare for. I'm only as good as my last task. But on that occasion at least, I remember thinking, job's a good 'un! I look back on the whole trip with such fondness. Since then, I've been to the United States a few times and have always been met with such a warm welcome, everywhere I've been.

The hat matches the lace collar and black buttons. We later trimmed the flower down a little for a lighter look.

'The State Visit of 2007 was the second time I welcomed Her Majesty to The White House. Weeks before The Queen arrived, I received a call from Her Majesty's Page, Barry Mitford, to discuss plans for the trip. I was struck by the vivid detail with which Her Majesty obviously recalled the floor plans and layout of The White House from her previous visit in 1991. Barry relayed that The Queen had met with his team and provided specific directions on where her luggage was to be placed and other logistical arrangements. Although he hadn't been there on this occasion, his directions were exact and spot on – Her Majesty is obviously observant of even the smallest details.

The 2007 visit was the first time I met Angela Kelly. I recall that within minutes of her arrival, Angela came to me with two specific directions. Firstly, Her Majesty wished that the Blair House staff should serve her and The Duke of Edinburgh – a kind gesture that gave our staff the honour of being near The Queen. Secondly, I would be required to accompany Her Majesty in the elevator each time she used it – not because The Queen was unfamiliar with which buttons to use, but again as a kind gesture to allow us to be in Her presence.

Angela Kelly was most gracious and allowed me to take a close look at several of Her Majesty's amazing pieces of jewellery. She told me that certain items belonged to Her Majesty's grandmother and that one in particular was a gift from her father, and I was entranced. It was also a wonderful opportunity to see some of Angela's own creations, such as the aquamarine ensemble Her Majesty wore to the Garden Party held at the British Embassy during that visit.

Her Majesty and The Duke of Edinburgh were delightful guests and had an uncanny way of making everyone around them feel at ease. On the last day of their visit, The Queen presented me with a framed signed photograph of herself and The Duke of Edinburgh. Moments after I left the room, a Palace official came to find me and indicated that Her Majesty thought I should receive another gift as she had remembered that I had received a photograph after their visit in 1991. I was overwhelmed by how thoughtful she was.'

By Randy Bumgardner

Blair House Manager

UNITED NATIONS TO GROUND ZERO

While on a Royal Tour, The Queen is often required to attend sensitive and sombre occasions among her engagements. Often, these events happen in close succession as Her Majesty's schedule can be very tight, and it is on these occasions that we put even more thought than usual into her outfits for the day.

In July 2010, The Queen was due to travel to New York and had been invited to attend two important events, one after the other. The first was a visit to the United Nations, where Her Majesty was asked to deliver a speech, fifty-three years after she had first addressed the UN in 1957 at the age of thirty-one. The second was a visit to Ground Zero, the site of the former Twin Towers of the World Trade Center, destroyed by terrorist attack on 11 September 2001. The Queen had been asked to lay a wreath.

From my perspective, designing something suitable for this occasion was a major challenge. The Queen would be moving from the very formal setting of the indoor auditorium at the United Nations to an outdoor event attended by bereaved families. Both events were serious, although very different in tone and mood, and Her Majesty would not have time to change outfits between them. I needed to find something that would be authoritative enough for Her Majesty's speech at the UN but not too severe and formal for the visit to Ground Zero. In terms of colouring, I needed something that would complement the imposing backdrop of the auditorium while allowing Her Majesty to stand out, but not overly vibrant considering her next engagement. In the end, I decided on a soft, floral material for the dress and jacket in muted blue, white, and metallic taupe. The edges of the jacket would be ruffled to suggest softness and femininity. I was pleased with the result and confident that it would be suitable for both events.

We arrived in New York to discover that the city was experiencing its worst heatwave in decades. The tarmac was melting onto the soles of

Opposite: The Queen on her visit to New York City in 2010.

people's shoes and the same was happening to ours! My immediate concern was that The Queen would be too hot with the long-sleeved jacket: thank goodness I had not opted for a heavier material! I needn't have worried, though: when I watched Her Majesty on television that day, her speech to the UN was calm and collected, and her presence at the Ground Zero wreath-laying ceremony provided comfort and reassurance to those who attended. It was a sad occasion and I couldn't help but reflect on my own good fortune. Although The Queen didn't say anything to me at the time, I could tell that she was deeply moved. We were all relieved when both engagements went smoothly and I was proud that Her Majesty's outfit had stood her in good stead.

When I first started designing, I used to buy the full roll so that no one else would be able to wear the same material, and would design multiple outfits from it. This silk material made a plain dress, a suit, a cocktail dress, and the trim for a cashmere coat. I am more thrifty now and just buy what is needed for the outfit I'm designing for specific occasions.

Left: The Queen lays a
wreath at the site of the
World Trade Center in
New York City in 2010.

AN IMPECCABLE HOST

I imagine that there aren't many people who have the privilege of being in the presence of multiple Presidents, but I am lucky to be one of them. On 3 June 2019, Her Majesty welcomed President Donald Trump to Buckingham Palace. Arriving by helicopter, he touched down on the lawn that just a few days before had been host to 8,000 guests at The Queen's last garden party of the spring. It was quite a surreal moment to watch the Presidential helicopter approach – I'm sure you can imagine that I was watching attentively from the window.

For State occasions like this, everything must run like clockwork, and on this one, thankfully, it did. As soon as the helicopter's rotors came to a rest, the President and the First Lady disembarked and the engagements began. The First Lady looked stunning and really set the tone for what turned out to be a very stylish visit. That evening, Her Majesty hosted a State Banquet in President Trump's honour and each and every guest looked fabulous. As always, it was an honour to dress The Queen for such an important occasion. I had chosen a beautiful gown decorated with fine lace and ornate beading of small daisies and crystals – we named this dress 'Daisy Chain'. Her Majesty wore this with the Garter Sash and Star, as well as the Burmese Ruby and Diamond Tiara, the ruby and diamond necklace, earrings, and bracelet, alongside her white gold watch and ruby diamond rings. The whole outfit was complemented beautifully by a silver handbag and matching silver shoes.

Throughout President Trump's visit, the media had many opportunities to take pictures, not only of the glamorous State Banquet but also of the ceremony to commemorate the seventy-fifth anniversary of the D-Day landing in Portsmouth. Preparing the outfit for this occasion took much consideration – Her Majesty needed to wear something special considering how many world leaders would be in attendance. In the end, I suggested a beautiful fuchsia coat, which, although striking in colour, was simple and elegant. Underneath, Her Majesty wore a floral-patterned dress and we accompanied it with a stunning cerise hat. On this occasion, choosing The Queen's jewellery was simple – I immediately knew that she should wear a brooch that has sentimental value for Her Majesty

A very stylish visit.

Opposite: The Queen with President Donald Trump at Buckingham Palace in 2019.

as she gifted it to her mother, Queen Elizabeth The Queen Mother, for her one-hundredth birthday. It would also complement the pink outfit.

As The Queen delivered her speech on that momentous occasion, standing next to the President of the United States, President Trump, I was reminded once again of how fortunate I am to be at her service and play a small part in dressing The Queen.

Close up of the Daisy Chain dress detail.

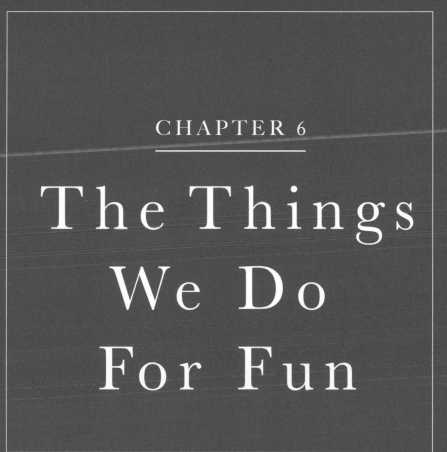

CHAPTER 6

The Things We Do For Fun

A SNEAKY PLAN

Her Majesty and I often have fun together, especially when we're away on a Royal Tour and I have the luxury of some spare time. Some time ago, in October 1996, Her Majesty went on a State Visit to Thailand and, as well as the beautiful landscape and stunning local scenery, one personal memory will stay with me for ever.

In the weeks leading up to that trip, I was preoccupied with preparing The Queen's outfits – on this occasion many vibrant lightweight silks because of the humid weather conditions – and I'd been so busy I'd simply run out of time to get to a hairdresser to refresh my roots. While I was reading the programme of engagements for the trip, I noticed there would be a market just across from the Royal Palace where we were to stay in Bangkok, and I mentioned to The Queen that I was planning to nip to a chemist in the market to buy a box of hair dye. I thought Ian Carmichael, The Queen's Hairdresser, should be able to colour my hair, no problem, while Her Majesty was out for a whole day on one of her engagements. The Queen was surprised by my plan, and insisted that it would be impossible because the box of hair colour would have no English instructions. I told her not to worry, and that it would be just fine, as the instructions are always the same, no matter what country you are in. I had to excuse myself quickly on that occasion so that The Queen did not see my smile – for I was coming up with a sneaky plan . . .

When we arrived in Thailand, it was just as humid as we'd anticipated but everyone was so friendly and accommodating that everything went smoothly. A couple of days into the tour, Her Majesty and The Duke of Edinburgh were due to attend a Royal Barge Procession of 2,000 oarsmen dressed in traditional costumes, manning fifty-two barges, watching from the banks of the Chao Phraya river, so I thought this would be the perfect time to carry out my plan. That morning, I told The Queen I was going to the market to collect my hair dye, and she again told me she thought it would be a big mistake. While Her Majesty was out at her engagements, and once I'd finished all my duties, I let Ian in on my cunning plan: I had no intention of getting my hair done in Thailand – I was there to work. Before we'd left England, though, I had been to Accessorize and found a vibrant purple hairpiece made with fake hair. Ian knows my sense of humour, so he was more than happy to help and we spent some time attaching it

Opposite: The Queen visits Thailand in 1996.

in various ways to my head, to make sure it looked as realistic as possible.

A few hours later, when The Queen returned from her engagement, she started to tell me enthusiastically about what a splendid time she'd had and all the interesting people she'd met. She did not notice my new purple hair, so I pulled the piece slightly further forward on my head, but Her Majesty still didn't notice and kept talking about her day. I realised I had to do something dramatic, so I waited until she'd stopped talking, turned with the most sorrowful look and said, 'Your Majesty! Look what's happened! Look at the colour of my hair!' I even started to pull the purple strands out, saying, 'Look, my hair is falling out!'

The Queen looked flabbergasted for a moment, then trying to contain her laughter, Her Majesty exclaimed, 'Ian! What have you done to her hair?!' Everyone heard the commotion but all I could do was laugh. The Queen was chuckling quietly to herself as she told me to go away. I'll never know how I got away with it, but Her Majesty has quite a sense of humour.

The Queen was chuckling quietly to herself as she told me to go away.

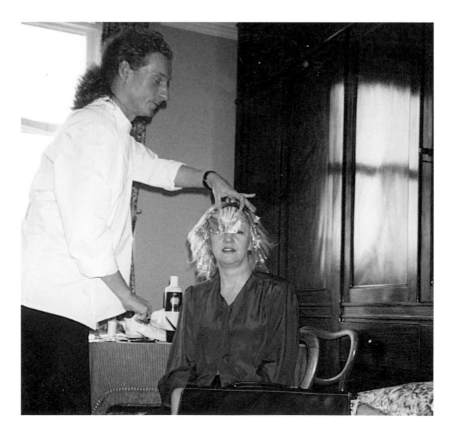

Ian Carmichael and me.

AN UNFORGETTABLE EXPERIENCE

When Her Majesty and The Duke of Edinburgh travel abroad for a Royal Tour, we members of the Royal Household usually have a hectic schedule and have to make sure that everything goes smoothly. However, that doesn't mean we can't have a little free time to ourselves, and often it's on these little solo trips that we have the best fun. Usually, I miss out on such things because someone has to be there in case Her Majesty needs something. There was one time, though, when I managed to have a little fun of my own.

It was October 1997, and The Queen was on a Royal visit to Pakistan and India, which turned out to be an incredible experience. The atmosphere in both countries was magical, with music always in the air and a vast array of vibrant outfits to be seen. Over one weekend some of the Royal staff had had the opportunity to see the Taj Mahal as no Royal events were scheduled. I, along with a couple of others from the Royal Household had to stay behind as we can't all go on these explorations. However, given that we would both have liked to see the Taj Mahal, The Queen asked the Page to arrange for us to go on another day. Unlike the rest of the staff, though, we would be travelling in a tiny plane. As we made our way on board, I could tell this plane had many uses and functions, from transporting people, to cargo and probably more I would never even imagine. We were lucky enough to fly to the mausoleum and spend the day there, soaking up the rich historic surroundings. The colours were beautiful, and it is a most moving memorial to the love that existed between Shah Jahan and his chief consort, Mumtaz Mahal, who died in 1631. It's impossible to see that magnificent structure without mulling over their story. Before we left, I went to the souvenir shop and bought a plate that would remind me of the Taj Mahal's shimmering marble walls and the wonderful adventure we had had that day.

Opposite: *The beautiful splendour of the Taj Mahal.*

A BIRD IN THE HAND

Having travelled so much, Her Majesty is the best tour guide ever, as she always takes the time to learn about the countries she visits. The Queen is full of interesting information and useful hints and tips. I never thought, in my wildest dreams, that I would have the chance to see Australia, so when we were preparing for my first Royal Tour there in 2006, I was so excited to hear about all the wildlife – the kangaroos we would see (red and grey), the koalas and dingoes. Her Majesty also mentioned the kookaburra and said that, although it is not the finest-looking bird, it makes a sound you will never forget. I asked if she thought I would see any, and Her Majesty replied, 'Oh, yes, many.'

The Royal Tour was going smoothly and we were all having a wonderful time. However, despite The Queen's confident response, I had not even heard a kookaburra, let alone seen one. I was a bit disappointed as I'd been so looking forward to seeing (and hearing!) the wildlife. Each time I heard an unusual bird call, I would turn to The Queen and ask her if that was the infamous call, and each time she said it was not.

One day, Her Majesty was due to visit the Sydney Opera House and the Harbour Bridge before a garden party to be held that afternoon in the grounds of the Governor's House, where we were staying. That morning, it was raining torrentially but, of course, The Queen would never let anyone down. After breakfast, she changed and left for the Opera House. As Her Majesty would be out all morning, the staff had an early lunch before we were all taken to the local indoor market. Walking around the stalls, I noticed that one vendor was selling birds. Among all the beautiful, brightly coloured ones I spotted a rather dull-looking brown bird and immediately thought that this must be the elusive kookaburra. I asked the shopkeeper, 'What is that unusual looking bird?' and she said, 'It's the Kookaburra.' So I bought it – I had something in mind that I thought The Queen would enjoy.

Back at the Governor's House, Her Majesty wasn't due to return for a little while so I went up to her room to find the perfect perch for my new friend. I thought it might enjoy sitting in the sunshine which had just come out after the rain that morning, as it was used to hot weather, so I placed it outside on the balcony in a little cage. I waited in The Queen's room for her to return and when she came in, and walked across the room, I said, 'Your Majesty, there's a funny-looking grey bird on your balcony.'

Without a pause, The Queen looked outside and shouted, 'It's a kookaburra!' I went to open the cage doors and she said loudly, 'No! Don't do that! It will fly away!' and was behind me in a flash. I went to the bird, picked it up and, turning to Her Majesty while trying to keep a straight face, I solemnly told her it was dead. She looked horrified as I walked towards her with outstretched arms and as she took the bird from my hands, she realised I had been winding her up all along. It was really a stuffed toy. 'April Fool!' I said, with a mischievous grin on my face and she had only two words for me: 'You're sacked!' I was laughing uncontrollably as Her Majesty turned to His Royal Highness, and said 'Do you know what she has just done to me? Angela has had me!' and I just couldn't stop giggling.

I never did get to see a real kookaburra, but I'm pleased to say that the toy I bought in the market that day is with us in Windsor Castle and has pride of place on the back of the sofa in The Queen's sitting room. I laugh to myself every time I see it.

'You're sacked'

Illustration by Sophia and
Serena Polycarpou.

WHAT A CORKER

When I reflect on the various Royal Tours I have been so lucky to attend, it strikes me that Australia always seems to bring out my mischievous side. Of course, Royal visits abroad involve lots of planning and preparation, but they also offer the opportunity for fun and jokes, and one particular memory from our second tour to the continent in 2011 will stay with me for ever.

The Queen and The Duke of Edinburgh were due to attend some rather unusual events on that Royal Tour, including a barbecue, a tram ride, and a rainforest walk in Brisbane, so I had several things to consider when preparing my new collection for The Queen to wear.

First and foremost, the weather would be a lot warmer there than it had been in London, so I wanted her outfits to be cool. This applied to the hats, too, and as I was researching, I remembered seeing photographs of Australians wearing hats with corks hanging from the brim – I think they might even be called cork hats! When I looked into this a bit more, I learned that the dangling corks were supposed to keep insects off your face. In a slightly mischievous mood, I decided to create an extra-special hat for Her Majesty to suit the occasion . . .

The journey to Australia went without a hitch and after we arrived at the Governor General's Residence, I began unpacking The Queen's luggage and helping her to prepare for her busy schedule. Aware that this was the day of the rainforest visit, I decided to present Her Majesty with two headwear options for the engagement. The first hat perfectly matched the dress, which was a Karl Ludwig creation made of satin silk in pinks and green with a pale green fine wool coat. The second was similar, with a crucial difference: it sported corks dangling from the brim. Eyeing the options, The Queen eventually looked up at me and asked, 'Why?' in a very matter-of-fact way. I explained that the corks might be of use in discouraging any flying insects from approaching her face. The Queen lifted the hat and pretended to put it on, laughing to herself. It's at a moment like that – sharing a joke with Her Majesty while on a visit to one of the most beautiful countries in the world – that I truly appreciate how lucky I am to work for someone with such a great sense of humour.

MEETING THE LOCALS

Over the years, I've visited some of the world's most amazing sights and most beautiful countries. Never in my wildest dreams did I expect to see the White House or the Taj Mahal, or the breathtaking mountain ranges of Canada. Before a Royal Tour overseas, I often have something in mind that I'd like to see there, should I have some free time, and during my second visit to Australia, I was determined to catch sight of a kangaroo. We were scheduled to be in the country for ten days – plenty of time, I thought, to spot one.

As the tour went on and we travelled across the magnificent landscapes, I had yet to catch a glimpse of one. As we made our way to Canberra, where we would be staying in Government House, I started to wonder if I would manage to see a kangaroo, having travelled all that way! I remember that it was the hottest weather I had ever experienced. The days passed, and as I went about my duties, I would pop my head out of the window now and again: perhaps I'd see something hopping along in the garden.

One day, Her Majesty was out on an engagement and all the staff were enjoying lunch. Everyone knew how much I wanted to see a kangaroo, so Barry Mitford, The Queen's Page, suggested that we all get changed into casual clothes and meet at the garden entrance to go kangaroo spotting. I had an idea: we should camouflage ourselves so that we could get as close as possible without being seen. So, like fools, a few of us scurried around and found twigs and leaves to put in our hair.

After quite some time roaming around, trying to locate the animals we had been assured lived in the grounds, we finally spotted something – I knew immediately from the large, powerful back legs and feet that it was a kangaroo! It was unlike any creature I'd seen before and I wanted to get a closer look. So we started crawling along the grass towards it, as though we were carrying out an army exercise, like Private Benjamin. I can't imagine what we must have looked like. As we inched closer, Barry told me to keep aware: kangaroos can be quite aggressive. I could now see that it was a male red kangaroo, the largest of all kangaroo species. He seemed to be quite preoccupied with the grass he was chewing, but I noticed he was also keeping a watchful eye on us. We were getting really quite close, around 5 metres away, when all of a sudden, he started pounding his foot on the ground. The noise was so loud that we all leaped up in a panic and I could hear Barry shouting that we should run. We scrambled back to the safety of the house, twigs flying from our hair. The kangaroo was clearly unimpressed and I'm sure he thought he was teaching us a lesson – it certainly worked!

Trying to blend in with the background.

CUTTING IT FINE

The Queen likes to support local people wherever she visits, but we have a particular little tradition whenever we go to Singapore. There's never enough time to go to the market, but as Her Majesty loves Singaporean silk, local tradespeople bring their stalls to the airport when she is due to arrive so that she can personally browse all that they have to offer.

We wander through the stalls – Her Majesty leading the way, followed by me and the Ladies-in-Waiting. Something will catch The Queen's eye – usually a particularly vibrant fabric, given her fondness for bright colours – and she'll make a gesture to me. Seeing lovely material like this is usually very inspiring and I'll quickly have an idea for a dress, a coat, a jacket, and maybe a hat – 5 metres should be enough. Her Majesty will point to another roll and I'll envisage a cocktail dress – 3 metres will be plenty. So, this is our routine: we amble around the stalls until we've found everything we're looking for, at which point, having placed our orders, we go off on the tour. Our selections are always ready for collection on our return, when it's my responsibility to pay the bill.

A few years ago, after Her Majesty's Ladies-in-Waiting and I had collected our parcels of silk, I went to make the payment and the stall owners advised me that I could claim tax back on the purchase. The Queen is always keen to keep costs down, so off I went in search of someone who could help. A few minutes later, as I was getting the tax back, another member of the Royal staff rushed up to me in a panic, shouting that we had to go straight away as the plane was leaving right that second. Soon I was running across the tarmac, flying up the steps to the plane just in time. I was so thrilled, I shouted over the plane's engines a phrase I am sure The Queen does not hear very often: 'I've got your tax back!' The look on The Queen's face was priceless as I handed her the tax refund.

WHEN THE PAST AND PRESENT COME TOGETHER

As well as all the events and work that gets done, there are also countless formal traditions that are upheld in the Royal Household, as well as some less formal ones that we members of staff look forward to each year. One, in particular, is a real favourite – a fancy-dress competition that is held twice a year at Balmoral, once in August and once in September so that everyone gets to take part. Balmoral Court is split into two halves, with a staff changeover at the start of September. Everyone goes to town for this one because, as part of the event, The Queen dresses in a beautiful evening gown and even wears a tiara – to judge the winners of first, second, and third place. Her family might join together to make a judging panel if they happen to be there too. As fancy-dress night approaches, many secret meetings are held around the Castle. Trips are made to fancy-dress stores and charity shops, and you'll find wigs and papier-mâché everywhere!

A couple of years ago, we decided to change things up a bit as The Queen was taking a short break from the judging and was having dinner with the Royal Family and guests on the evening of the event. Of course, no one can replace Her Majesty, but we decided it would be fitting to have four 'famous' judges instead: members of the Household dressed up as Louis Walsh, Nicole Scherzinger and Simon Cowell, while I was to be Cheryl Cole. We even elected a compère to host the evening and announce the guests. But, of course, we still had our jobs to do. On the morning of the competition, I asked Her Majesty if she would mind that her dressers would be in fancy dress when they attended to her later that day – as we didn't want to be too late for our party. Without hesitation, The Queen said, 'No, no, no, you must!'. So we went about preparing our outfits and readying ourselves for the night ahead.

You can only imagine the look on The Queen's face when she saw me that evening wearing a red military jacket, black leather boots and a long, dark wig. She didn't have a clue who I was supposed to be, but she immediately

Opposite: *Alone with my thoughts in the Castle grounds.*

recognised my assistant, Jackie, who was dressed as . . . Her Majesty's great-great-grandmother, Queen Victoria. Alongside Queen Victoria, our other dresser was made up as Victoria's close friend and supporter, John Brown. That year the theme for the fancy dress was 'Balmoral', so the staff had dressed up as various people and animals associated with the estate.

Jackie had put in so much effort, even searching online for tips on how to style her hair correctly, but she felt embarrassed as she stood there, wearing all black with her hair in plaited buns, before The Queen. But it went down a treat with Her Majesty. Just before she left for her dinner, she said, 'I suppose I'll see you tomorrow,' suggesting that we might all be suffering from slightly sore heads the next day. Then, on her way down the stairs, we heard her exclaim to her guests: 'I've just been dressed by Queen Victoria and Mr Brown! I've been dressed by Queen Victoria herself, and John Brown. And I believe by Cheryl Cole!' Just to add to Jackie's embarrassment, later that evening as she was doing a walkabout with other staff members in fancy dress, presenting her outfit to me and the other judges, her hand resting on 'John Brown's' arm, the door opened and there were three guests from The Queen's dinner taking pictures! We must have been quite the discussion point at dinner.

Jackie as Queen Victoria, with me as Cheryl Cole!

'I've just been dressed by Queen Victoria herself'

CONCLUSION

Dear Reader

Writing this book has been a humbling experience. This is not a piece of historical writing, but an amazing journey and the absolutely true facts of living and working with The Queen over the last twenty-five years – long may it continue.

This experience has taught me many things, particularly having patience with myself; while continuing to serve Her Majesty The Queen, and fulfilling all my duties to the high standard I set myself, I have managed to write this book alongside my daily working life.

It was a joy to reminisce with The Queen over these stories and now having the honour of sharing them with you. The Queen was with me every step of the way.

Though my beginnings were humble, it took me many years to believe in myself – to have the courage and determination to make something of myself.

There have been many changes since my early years in the Royal Household. For example, it is not a man's world any more; it is a fabulous professional working environment for men and women in Buckingham Palace today. I get to work with some of the most talented, kind, and inspiring people.

I hope this book has given you the inspiration and courage to follow your dreams like I did. My wish for you is that they all come true.

Thank you for reading my book and I hope we meet again . . . until next time.

Love, Angela Kelly
X

'Since meeting Angela eleven years ago, my life has never been the same. Working for her on the Dressers' Floor has been a joy and a privilege.

Angela fills me with confidence and is always so positive and enthusiastic that it rubs off on me and makes me feel like I can achieve anything.

She is warm, funny, and has a big heart, but when it comes to reaching deadlines, she puts her serious head on and will always find a way to solve any problem. She is great to work for and we have mutual respect for each other.'

Stella

'It is an honour to work for Her Majesty and alongside Miss Kelly, one of the designers responsible for turning The Queen into a fashion icon all across the globe. Miss Kelly's loyalty to her job is a constant inspiration to us. She is a generous and fun-loving Mother Hen to our Dressers' Floor family.'

The Dressers

'When asked to write a brief paragraph or two about my working relationship with Angela, I thought to myself, Where do I start?.

When you have worked and travelled around the globe with the most famous person in the world for more than twenty years, it can never be anything less than an honour – full of excitement and memories to keep for ever.

Working with Angela and seeing her in action is quite amazing to witness. She is a total professional, through and through.

I have been extremely lucky to have known Angela as a dear friend and I'm sure she will agree that we have had many, many great laughs together.

This is a lady with an amazing sense of humour who is not afraid to laugh at herself, but most of all has great interest in the needs of others, which I simply adore.

She is a pleasure to work with and I pray that we have many more years together of working hard and laughing hard.'

Ian Carmichael

'My working relationship with Angela began about eighteen years ago.

I joined the Royal Household in 2001 and was working in a different department. It wasn't long before I heard the name "Angela Kelly" mentioned and that she was a woman not to be messed with.

Needless to say, I expected the worst when we first met while I was undertaking luggage duties.

The truth was quite different. I met Angela and the rest of her team and everyone was very welcoming. Over the years, as I performed my luggage duties, I built up a relationship with Angela.

Angela guards The Queen's privacy relentlessly and this crosses over into her personal domain. If Angela needed any duties seen to in her private rooms, I was among one of the few people she trusted.

This all changed in early 2018 when, unbeknown to myself, I was being headhunted by Angela. I headed up to the Dressers' Floor one day to undertake a job. Before I knew it, we were in discussions about me joining the team. I was stunned to say the least.

So, here we are eighteen months later and I am Project Manager for our department, among many other duties. I am deeply grateful to Angela for seeing something in me that she wanted to bring to her team.

Angela is a wonderful boss and a pleasure to work for. Yes, we have our busy days when we have to knuckle down, but Angela always tries to make it fun and keep everyone's spirits high.

I may have only been with the team a short time but I have been made to feel very much part of that team. During this time, I have noticed how Angela is a good friend to those close to her and loyal to the core.

I have yet to meet the formidable woman I was warned of so many years ago.

Working with Angela is a pleasure and I will be eternally grateful for the many exciting opportunities she has given me.'

Neil

'After working for the Royal Household as the Administrator for the F Branch Office (Catering) for ten years, I became Angela's Personal Assistant on 12 August 2013.

I love being a part of the team on the Dressers' Floor. If you were to come up and visit us, you would hear laughter coming from the workroom, music playing quietly in the background and you would hear the girls singing away (they have great voices, by the way!), and that would all be happening before eight in the morning! Then you would hear, "Morning, girls" and there would be Angela all set and raring for the day to start. She is always good to go!

Angela is an amazing manager and boss – although both words are a struggle for me to use as Angela is more like your best friend. Angela has always supported my decisions, even if on the odd occasion they haven't been the best ones; she will always have my back. The love she has for her family shows every time we talk about them. She does have rather a soft spot for her grandchildren! Angela is so incredibly loyal and has allowed me to share with her some amazing adventures. From travelling to New York City to meet with Annie Leibovitz, to almost missing our train coming back from Glamis Castle, to also being trained as an Assistant Dresser and being able to revisit Balmoral Castle and Sandringham House.

It has been on these occasions, travelling as an Assistant Dresser, when I have seen Angela and Her Majesty interact with each other and I have been able to see their unique relationship shine through. I have experienced so much laughter on these occasions. I mean, come on, I dressed up for our evening duties as Queen Victoria! I will never forget that evening when The Queen saw us all and shared a laugh with us about it.

There was also a time when I was waiting for Angela, who was helping The Queen get ready for the State Banquet during a State Visit. In the reflection of the mirror, I could see Angela helping The Queen secure the tiara onto her head, all the while hearing the banter and laughter being shared. It was definitely a "pinch-yourself" moment for me when I curtsied to The Queen as she passed me to leave the room.

Never would I have thought that this small-town girl from Maine, USA, would ever be in the position that I am in today. Thank you, Angela! Long may our crazy, fun adventures continue.

I truly hope you will be able to get a sense of Angela's warmth, dedication, and the commitment she has as the Personal Advisor to The Queen, and that you will also be able to imagine that you are in the same room experiencing the laughter that is shared between Her Majesty The Queen and Angela as you read this book.'

Jackie Newbold MVO

ACKNOWLEDGEMENTS

Your Majesty, I would like to personally thank you for giving me your permission and blessing to write this book. I also thank you for your guidance and advice. Thank you for putting up with me for all the times when I have gone back and forth to you, checking and double-checking the stories. I am truly thankful for the time you gave me and for allowing me to share this book with the world. I am your humble servant.

To my children and grandchildren, once again I thank you for your continued love and support. I am forever grateful to you for understanding the way I balance my working life with the special times that I spend with you. Special thanks to Jacob Wylie for helping me finalise the book.

I would like to thank June Anson for not only being a part of my family but for your friendship, company, and loyalty.

I would also like to thank Paul and Margaret Grayson who have not just been part of my family but have been my closest friends. Thank you for your constant support, friendship, and loyalty.

Elizabeth Sheinkman, you have been my protector and my guardian and I thank you from the bottom of my heart for helping this book come alive and for making sure the working relationship and the magical moments were truly represented.

My gratitude and thanks go to you all at HarperCollins for making this book beautiful, elegant, and regal. The hard work that has gone into this book has been outstanding. Firstly, I would like to give a special thanks to Katya Shipster, Zoe Berville, Lucy Brown, and Claire Ward for working tirelessly to help and support me. You have all gone beyond the call of duty. I would also like to thank: Abi Hartshorne, James Empringham, Georgina Atsiaris, Sarah Hammond, Sarah Burke, Fiona Greenway, Liane Payne, Fionnuala Barrett, Josie Turner, Dawn Burnett, Tom Dunstan, Anna Derkacz, Hazel Orme, and Helena Caldon. I would also like to thank Jonathan Burnham and Lisa Sharkey from the US branch of HarperCollins. It was wonderful to share the same enthusiasm and excitement. Thank you for fully understanding the sensitivity and the discretion that surrounded this book.

To do the audio recording of this book terrified me! Thanks, therefore, to Alex at ID Studio, who encouraged me, and kept me calm and within the hours. We had a great understanding and a great working relationship which made the audio a success.

I would like to thank the members of the Royal Household (too many to name individually) as you have been great supporters and advisors which has helped to make this unique book so special.

Thank you to the Royal Collection for your co-operation, especially Tim Knox, who has been a great supporter from the first time we were introduced.

I would like to thank you, Samantha Cohen, for all your hard work and support you have given me, not only with my first book, *Dressing The Queen*, but also with this book. You have been my constant supporter from the first day we met many, many years ago. I truly value our friendship and our working relationship.

Michael Atmore, I would like to thank you for your professionalism, for your help and guidance. Your constant support has been vital and I appreciate you being there for me day and night. You have gone above and beyond what anyone could ever ask for. I am so proud to call you my friend.

The team on the Dressers' Floor has a unique bond, just like a small family. Your support that you give me makes my work so much easier so I am able to look after The Queen. I really appreciate all your hard work. You truly are the crème de la crème!

Thank you to all the photographers for allowing me to use your beautiful photographs and for the wonderful contribution you have made to make this book so special. A picture says a thousand words! I would like to say a special thank you to Eva Zielinska-Millar for your advice and guidance.

Andy and Sharon Polycarpou – I would like to thank you for allowing your two beautiful daughters, Serena and Sophia, to spend time with me discussing the illustrations for this book. They are two very talented girls. Serena and Sophia – I would like to thank you for putting my vision to paper and for contributing to this book and making it beautiful. I know it was a busy time for you as you were still in school, so thank you for finding time for me. May I wish you all the best for future. Don't let your talent go to waste. You are both an inspiration to all young people.

David Morgan-Hewitt at The Goring hotel: although you did not know I was writing this book, our friendship, over the many years, has meant so much to me. You are a true friend and I have enjoyed your company. I look forward to our next dinner, whenever our busy schedules allow it.

Jackie Newbold, there are so many things I would like to thank you for, but too numerous to mention them all. I do want to thank you for your endless support as a true friend. You astound me with your calmness, patience, and determination to help bring this book together with me. Thank you for putting up with me and for all of my changes, making sure I got it right. With your help and support you never gave up on me. You believed in me and helped make this book what it is today. I could not have done this without you.

A special thanks and gratitude goes to you, the reader. I do hope you enjoyed reading my book and that, once again, you caught a glimpse of this magical world. I hope you cherish this book, like I cherish my memories.

With love, Angela x

HarperCollins*Publishers*
1 London Bridge Street
London SE1 9GF

www.harpercollins.co.uk

First published by HarperCollins*Publishers* 2019

10 9 8 7 6 5

A catalogue record of this book is available from the British Library

ISBN 978-0-00-836836-4

Printed and bound Bell and Bain Ltd, Glasgow

Picture credits